PERU
PATHS TO POVERTY

Latin America Bureau

Special Brief

First published in Great Britain in 1985 by

Latin America Bureau (Research and Action) Limited
1 Amwell Street
London EC1R 1UL

Copyright © Latin America Bureau (Research and Action) Limited
1985

British Library Cataloguing in Publication Data

Reid, Michael
    Peru: paths to poverty.
    1. Peru — Economic conditions — 1968 —
    I. Title
    330.985'0633   HC227

ISBN 0-906156-22-X

Written by Michael Reid
Maps by Michael Green
Cover photo by Jenny Matthews/Format
Cover design by Chris Hudson
Typeset, printed and bound by Russell Press Ltd, Nottingham
Trade distribution in UK by Third World Publications

Erratum: The figure for full employment, page 2, should read 40%, not 30%.

Contents

Maps   iv

1. **Peru in Brief**   1

2. **Colony and Republic**   17

3. **The Birth of Mass Politics**   28

4. **Military Reformism**   42

5. **The System in Crisis**   54

6. **Political Democracy and Economic Disaster**   81

7. **Sendero Luminoso**   106

Appendices

1. **Structure of Production, 1978-1983**   128

2. **Real Income, 1978-1983**   128

3. **Election Results, 1980 and 1983**   129

COLOMBIA

ECUADOR

Tumbes
TUMBES

PIURA
Piura

Chiclayo

LAMBAYEQUE

Trujillo

Chimbote
ANCASH

PACIFIC OCEAN

CAJAMARCA
CAJAMARCA

AMAZONAS
Chachapoyas

SAN MARTIN
Moyobamba

LA LIBERTAD

Huaras

HUÁNUCO

Huánuco

PASCO
Cerro de Pasco

Iquitos

R. Marañón

LORETO

BRAZIL

CORDILLERA
ORIENTAL

CUZCO

MADRE DE DIOS

Maldonado

LIMA
LIMA

Callao
CALLAO

CORDILLERA
OCCIDENTAL

Pisco

JUNÍN

Huancayo

Huancavelica

HUAN-
CAVELICA

Ica

ICA

Puquio

Ayacucho
AYACUCHO

Abancay

APURI-
MAC

AREQUIPA

Machu
Picchu

Cuzco

Ayavin

PUNO

Lake
Titicaca

Puno

PUNO

Arequipa

Moquegua

MOQUEGUA

TACNA

Tacna

Arica

BOLIVIA

CHILE

Peru
Political

Kilometres
0   300

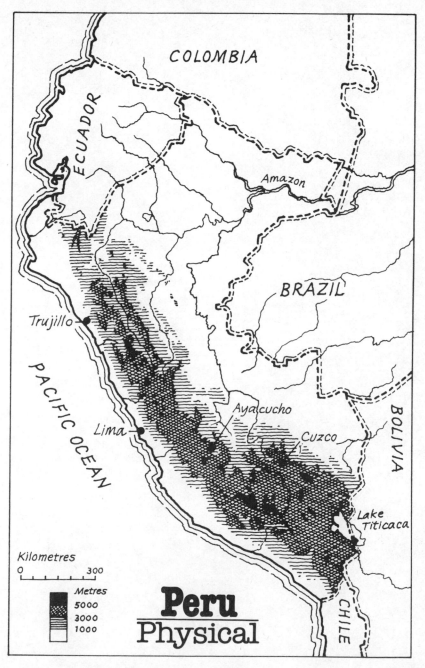

COLOMBIA

ECUADOR

Amazon

BRAZIL

PACIFIC OCEAN

Trujillo •

Lima •

Ayacucho

Cuzco

BOLIVIA

Lake
Titicaca

CHILE

Kilometres

0   300

Metres
5000
3000
1000

Peru
Physical

1 Peru in Brief

Statistics

Area   1,285,215 sq km

Population   Total 17.7 million (1981)
Growth 2.5% (annual average 1972-81)
Urban 1940 35%
       1961 47%
       1972 59%
       1981 66%

Principal Cities (1981)

Lima (including Callao)	4.9 million
Arequipa	447,000
Trujillo	354,000
Chiclayo	280,000
Chimbote	216,000
Piura	186,000
Cusco	182,000
Iquitos	173,000
Huancayo	165,000

The People   Origins   Amerindian 49%; Mixed 33%; White 12%; African and Mulatto 6%. The largest indigenous ethnic groups are: Quechua (8.2 million); Aymara (250,000); Campa (45,000); Shipibo (20,000); Cocama (20,000); Aguaruna (20,000).

Language	Spanish and Quechua are official languages. The 300,000 jungle indians are divided into 20 linguistic groups with over 50 distinct dialects.
Religion	Predominantly Roman Catholic, but evangelical protestants are estimated to number 700,000.
Adult literacy	1961 61.1%
	1972 72.5%
	1981 82.6%
Health	Life expectancy at birth 58 years (rural population 49 years) (1981). Infant mortality per thousand live births 101 (official 1981 figure).

The Economy GDP total US$19.5 billion

GDP growth 1970-74 annual average   6.3%.
1975-76 annual average   3.2%.
1977-78 annual average − 1.5%
1979   3.8%
1980   3.0%
1981   3.1%
1982   0.7%
1983 − 11.9%

GDP per capita US$1,070 (1983)

Income distribution (1972) percentage of income received by top
20% of households — 61.0%; lowest 20% —
1.9%; lowest 40%—7.0%

Inflation   1981   72.7%
1982   72.9%
1983 125.1%

Employment 30% of the economically active
population fully employed (1983)

Trade

	US$billion	
	Exports	Imports
1978	2.0	1.7
1979	3.7	2.0
1980	3.9	3.1
1981	3.2	3.8
1982	3.2	3.8
1983	3.0	2.7

Exports	Manufactured goods (mainly textiles, metal goods, fish products, chemicals) 18.4%; oil 18.0%; copper 14.7%; silver 13.0%; zinc 10.2%; lead 9.7%; coffee 3.9%; iron ore 2.5% (1983)
Major Trading Partners	Exports to US 34%; Japan 12.4%; West Germany 4.3%; Italy 3.5%; UK 3.3%. Imports from US 36%; Japan 9%; West Germany 8%; Brazil 4.8%; Argentina 3.5%; UK 2.5% (1978-82 average)
Foreign Direct Investment	US 48.8%; Switzerland 13.1%; Panama 8.9%; Italy 3.8%; UK 3.4% (stock in 1982)

Foreign Debt

	US$billion	%GDP
1970	3.7	59
1971	3.7	54
1972	3.8	50
1973	4.1	44
1974	5.2	45
1975	6.3	45
1976	7.4	54
1977	8.6	68
1978	9.3	87
1979	9.3	68
1980	9.6	56
1981	9.6	48
1982	11.1	56
1983	12.4	77

Debt Service (% export earnings) 1982 54%; 1983 44%

State Spending Education 12.1%; Health 4.1%; Defence 24% (1982)

Sources: Banco Central de la Reserva; Consejo Nacional de Poblacion; Comision Nacional de Inversiones y Tecnologias Extranjeras; Instituto Nacional de Estadisticas; World Bank.

A Note on Geography

Peru is the third largest country in South America, yet only 15 per cent of its land area is useable for agricultural purposes, and its dramatic

3

and difficult topography has impeded national integration and development. The country is divided into three main natural regions. The coastal plain is a narrow strip of desert, watered by 36 rivers whose valleys have been turned into fertile oases. The coastal region accounts for only eleven per cent of Peru's land area but contains half the population. Rising sharply from the coastal desert, the massive ranges of the Andes (whose highest peak is the 22,205ft Huascaran in Ancash's Cordillera Blanca) cover more than a quarter of the country. The high western cordillera of the Andes has created an unfortunate hydrological division: barely a hundred miles inland from the Pacific coast all the rivers form part of the Atlantic-flowing Amazon system. Until 1940 two out of three Peruvians lived in the highland (sierra) region, but subsequent migration has reduced this to 39 per cent. This population is crowded into deep valleys carved into the rocky massifs and inter-montane basins (altiplanos) of high altitude rough pasture. Only 4.5 per cent of the sierra is cultivable, while about a quarter is grazing land, largely of poor quality. East of the Andes lies the immense tropical rain forest of the Andean basin, accounting for almost two thirds of Peru's land area, but containing only eleven per cent of the population. Most of the population and the cultivable land in the jungle region is concentrated in the ceje de selva ('the eyebrow of the jungle') — a sub-region formed by the eastern Andean foothills and the broad tropical valleys which divide them.

Chronology

1532	Pizarro lands at Tumbes.
1780	Popular uprising under the leadership of Tupac Amaru, based in Cusco.
1821	July 28 — Declaration of independence from Spain by General San Martin.
1826-65	Era of military caudillos.
1840-80	Guano boom years.
1879-83	War of the Pacific against Chile.
1895-1919	'Aristocratic Republic' of elected governments of the oligarchy.
1924	APRA founded.
1930	PCP founded; Colonel Sanchez Cerro takes power in coup, repressing the labour movement.

1932	July — APRA uprising in Trujillo, in which officers are killed, is crushed with great brutality by the army.
1948-56	Dictatorship of General Manuel Odria upholds the rule of the oligarchy.
1956-62	Government of conservative civilian Manuel Prado.
1962	Stalemate in elections between Victor Raul Haya de la Torre (APRA) and Fernando Belaunde Terry (Accion Popular) leads to military coup and convoking of fresh elections by army junta; collapse of ELN rural guerrilla in Madre de Dios.
1963	Belaunde wins elections and presides over mildly reformist administration.
1965	MIR rural guerrilla fails in Junin and La Convencion.
1968	October — bloodless coup led by General Juan Velasco Alvarado ousts Belaunde; Velasco presides over strong military regime until 1975, introducing a series of major socio-economic reforms.
1975	February — deteriorating economic situation leads to riots in Lima during a police strike; 200 people killed. August — Velasco overthrown in bloodless coup led by General Francisco Morales Bermudez, who consolidates the regime's shift to the right; principal supporters of Velasco are retired from the armed forces; orthodox economic stabilisation policies introduced.
1976	June — wave of strikes against deflationary policies and devaluation of the currency (the sol); state of emergency declared and leading members of the opposition jailed or exiled.
1977	June — further series of price rises provokes widespread social discontent. July 19 — national general strike paralyses country. July 28 — Morales Bermudez announces timetable for return to civilian rule and lifts state of siege.
1978	February 27 and 28 — general strike fails to force reversal of redundancies. May — teachers' union SUTEP strikes for 81 days. May 22 and 23 — general strike; state of emergency declared and left-wing leaders exiled. June 18 — elections for Constituent Assembly; APRA wins greatest single representation but the left receives

30 per cent of the vote.

1979   January 9 — three-day general strike for reinstatement of redundant workers fails to achieve objective.

June — SUTEP stages national strike for wage rise; action finally called off in September without major success.

July — new Constitution ratified by Assembly; Haya de la Torre dies.

1980   May — general elections won by Belaunde and Accion Popular; the left's vote collapses; Sendero Luminoso stage first armed action in the department of Ayacucho; Belaunde administration begins to apply liberal policies and implement harsh deflation.

July — formation of Izquierda Unida left-wing alliance; APRA splits at party congress.

November — municipal elections show continued support for Accion Popular.

1981   January — government removes many price subsidies, provoking one-day general strike (15th).

April — decree no.46 introduced making it a crime to express support for Sendero.

September 22 — general strike against economic policies fails to generate mass support.

October — state of emergency declared in five provinces around town of Ayacucho; 701 armed actions by Sendero reported in 1981.

1982   March — Sendero occupy town of Ayacucho for a night.

May — new IMF loan agreed.

September — mass participation in Ayacucho funeral of leading senderista Edith Lagos, killed by security forces.

December — seven provinces in Ayacucho declared to be an emergency zone under military administration, led by General Clemente Noel.

1983   January 26 — eight journalists murdered in village of Uchuraccay, department of Ayacucho, leading to widespread suspicion that they were killed on military orders by local peasants; government-appointed commission led by novelist Mario Vargas Llosa later issues report largely favourable to the military; Sendero launches series of attacks, including the cutting of

Lima's electricity supply, which becomes a recurrent tactic.

March 10 — general strike against Belaunde's economic policy gains broad support.

August — Amnesty International sends open letter to Belaunde protesting at violation of human rights, particularly in Ayacucho, Belaunde vehemently rejects Amnesty's findings.

September — strike called by CGTP fails to make an impact.

November — Izquierda Unida wins municipal election in Lima; Alfonso Barrantes becomes the city's first left-wing mayor.

December — a total of eleven provinces in Ayacucho are now under direct military rule.

1984   March — one-day general strike by all unions.

July — military given overall charge of operations against Sendero; repression increases.

August — 50 bodies found in mass grave in Ayacucho; widespread belief that the massacre was perpetrated by the military.

Political Parties

In 1984 there were four main electoral forces in Peruvian politics.

1. Partido Popular Cristiano (PPC)

A right-wing party formed in 1966 when lawyer Luis Bedoya Reyes and other conservatives split from the more progressive Partido Democrata Cristiano (PDC). The PPC draws its support chiefly from industrialists and the Lima upper middle class. It was the minor partner in a coalition government with Accion Popular (AP) from 1980 until April 1984.

2. Accion Popular (AP)

Formed in 1956 after the presidential candidature of Arequipa architect Fernando Belaunde Terry, AP began as a reformist party of the provincial middle class, committed to the development of Peru

7

into a modern industrialised society through state planning and public works within the framework of a mixed economy. Belaunde was elected president in 1963 and again in 1980. By the 1980s the party had evolved towards a moderate conservatism.

AP's electoral success owed much to Belaunde's personal charisma and ability to draw votes from all social classes and regions. The unpopular record of his current government, and Belaunde's age (73) mean that his party's recent dominance of Peruvian electoral politics is unlikely to continue. Other leaders: Javier Alva Orlandini, Manuel Ulloa.

3. Partido Aprista Peruano (APRA)

The Partido Aprista Peruano (PAP) was founded in 1930 by former student leader Victor Raul Haya de la Torre. It is Peru's oldest and best organised political party although it has never governed the country. The PAP is technically the Peruvian section of a continent-wide APRA (Alianza Popular Revolucionaria Americana), founded by Haya de la Torre when exiled in Mexico in 1924, but the movement never spread beyond Peru.

APRA evolved from a populist nationalism in the 1930s — which provoked a fifty year feud with the army — to a conservative, pro-US stance in the 1950s and 1960s. The death of Haya in 1979 opened a prolonged internal struggle over the party's political line and leadership. This was resolved in 1982 with the election of Alan Garcia as general secretary, with the support of APRA's conservative leaders. Garcia has steered the party towards a moderate social democracy. An associate member of the Socialist International, APRA has particularly close links with Venezuela's Accion Democratica. APRA's traditional social base is amongst the lower middle class of the northern coast, but it also enjoys significant working class and some business support. Other leaders: Luis Alberto Sanchez, Armando Villanueva.

4. Izquierda Unida (IU)

IU was formed after divisions on the left resulted in disaster in the 1980 presidential elections. Its president is Alfonso Barrantes, a labour lawyer and non-aligned marxist. He was elected mayor of Lima in 1983. IU is a front of the following political parties:

Partido Comunista Peruano — 'Unidad' (PC-U)

The Peruvian Socialist Party was formed by Jose Carlos Mariategui and seven colleagues in 1928. In 1930, following Mariategui's death, the party affiliated to the Third International and changed its name to the PCP. To distinguish it from other fractions descended from the original party, the Moscow-line PC-U is popularly identified by the name of its weekly paper (*'Unidad'*). Although relatively small, the PC-U has the strongest working class base on the left. General Secretary: Jorge del Prado.

Unidad Democratica Popular (UDP)

Itself a front inside IU, the UDP was formed in 1977. Its main components were:

Movimiento de la Izquierda Revolucionaria (MIR)

The MIR was formed by radical ex-Apristas who, influenced by the success of the Cuban revolution and APRA's sharp rightward shift, left the party in 1959. They founded 'Apra Rebelde', which in 1962 changed its name to the MIR. Under the leadership of Luis De la Puente Uceda, the MIR staged an abortive rural guerrilla action in 1965. This resulted in De La Puente's death and the repression and division of the party. Several of the major tendencies reconstituted themselves in the 1970s as MIR-Unificado, which was a founding member of the UDP. General Secretary: Carlos Tapia.

Vanguardia Revolucionaria (VR)

VR was formed in 1965 when a group of revolutionary intellectuals linked up with a fraction of the MIR and dissident elements of Accion Popular. VR developed an independent marxist position drawing heavily on Mariategui's insistence on the need for a distinctively Peruvian socialism. Together with the PC-U and Patria Roja, VR is one of the larger parties on the left, with a dominant position in the CCP campesino federation and the miners' federation. General Secretary: Javier Diez Canseco.

In 1984, MIR and VR, together with the bulk of the PCR, formed the **Partido Unificado Mariateguista (PUM),** and UDP was effectively dissolved. The PUM has considerable support among students and intellectuals, as well as trade union and campesino leaders.

9

Partido Comunista Revolucionaria (PCR)

Formed in 1975, when a group, mainly composed of radical catholic youth and students, split from VR. After a further split, the majority of the PCR (known as Clase Obrera) supported UNIR (see below) in the 1980 elections. In 1984, the bulk of Clase Obrera joined the PUM, leaving an independent rump around General Secretary Manuel Dammert.

Union Nacional de la Izquierda Revolucionaria (UNIR)

UNIR was formed as a front to contest the 1980 presidential elections and later became a part of IU. Its most important member is:

Partido Comunista del Peru — Patria Roja

An orthodox pro-Peking maoist party, Patria Roja's roots go back to the Sino-Soviet split of 1964, when the maoist-sympathising campesino and youth sections of the PCP split and formed the PCP Bandera Roja, under the leadership of lawyer Saturnino Paredes. In a confused series of schisms between 1968 and 1970, a group calling itself the Comite Nacional Coordinadora left the by then pro-Albanian Bandera Roja. The dissident group subsequently changing its name to Patria Roja.

Patria Roja has an important base of support in the teachers union (SUTEP), which it controls, as well as supporters in campesino and student organisations. Unlike other members of IU, a large part of Patria Roja's membership remained in clandestinity following the return to civilian rule in 1980. General Secretary: Alberto Moreno.

Frente Obrero Campesino Estudantil y Popular (FOCEP)

Formed in 1963 by lawyer Genaro Ledesma and novelist Manuel Scorza, both of whom had assisted the campesinos of the central sierra in their struggles against the Cerro de Pasco Corporation and other landowners. In 1978, Ledesma formed an alliance with the trotskyist PST and POMR parties (see below). Running under the name of FOCEP, these combined forces won 12 per cent of the vote in the constituent assembly elections, largely because of the charismatic presence of the trotskyist Hugo Blanco. The trotskyists left FOCEP in 1980, and the rump around Ledesma that joined IU has little support outside Cerro de Pasco.

Partido Socialista Revolucionaria (PSR)

Founded in 1976 by progressive retired military officers and their civilian allies who had been identified with the more radical reforms of the government of General Juan Velasco. The PSR split shortly after the constituent assembly elections, its left-wing (PSR-ML) attaching itself to the UDP. The party retains a controlling presence in the CNA campesino organisation. The election of university teacher Enrique Bernales as secretary general following a further split in 1982 consolidated the PSR's evolution towards a left social-democrat position.

Other Parties

Sendero Luminoso

Formed in 1970 out of the Ayacucho regional committee and other fractions of Bandera Roja, Sendero's full name is 'Partido Comunista del Peru — Por El Sendero Luminoso de Jose Carlos Mariategui'. After establishing a base in Ayacucho's university and the surrounding campesino communities, Sendero began armed action in 1980. Using a maoist strategy of rural insurgency, combined with urban terrorism, Sendero was by 1984 waging a full-scale guerrilla war. During 1983 it formed a People's Revolutionary Army with an estimated strength of 2,500-3,000, supported by a rural militia and urban cells. Its major base of support is in Ayacucho and surrounding areas of the south-central sierra, but it also established a presence in Lima, Arequipa and the central jungle. Sendero is led by former philosophy teacher Abimael Guzman ('Camarada Gonzalo'). Sendero's armed insurgency has gained the support of a number of small groups:

Vanguardia Revolucionaria-Proletaria Comunista under Julio Cesar Mezzich, who as a VR member led mass campesino land invasions in Andahuaylas in 1974. Mezzich's group is believed to have merged with Sendero.

MIR-Cuarta Etapa, which began armed action in the northern sierra in 1983.

Puka Llacta, a dissident fraction of Patria Roja with support in the mining region around La Oroya and Cerro de Pasco. Puka Llacta has itself split into three fractions, one of which is engaged in armed action alongside Sendero.

PSR-Marxista Leninista. After supporting the UDP in the 1980 elections, some of the PSR-ML went underground. They began urban guerrilla actions in Lima in 1983.

Trotskyist Parties

There are three main trotskyist parties in Peru, none of which is large. The Partido Obrero Marxista Revolucionaria (POMR) was formed in 1971 by ex-VR leader Ricardo Napuri. The Partido Socialista de los Trabajadores (PST) was formed in 1974 when the previous Frente de Izquierda Revolucionaria of Hugo Blanco changed its name. In 1978 Blanco left to form the Partido Revolucionario de los Trabajadores (PRT). Both the PST (general secretary: Enrique Fernandez) and the PRT are aligned with the Unified Secretariat of the Fourth International. In the 1980 elections PRT, PST and POMR ran together under the name of the PRT.

Partido Democrata Cristiano (PDC)

Formed in 1956 by a group of intellectuals with its stronghold in Arequipa, the PDC never achieved the broad support gained by AP, with which it shared a reformist nationalism. After supporting the Belaunde government until 1966, PDC members were closely identified with the reforms of the Velasco government. Weakened by the exit of its right wing, which formed the PPC in 1966, as well as by its involvement with the military government, the PDC's following had become tiny by the 1980s.

Partido Hayista

In 1980, right-winger Andres Townsend walked out of APRA after failing to dislodge supporters of his rival Armando Villanueva from control of the party machine. The party has failed to achieve significant support beyond a section of the CTP trade union federation.

Frente Nacional de Trabajadores y Campesinos (FRENATRACA)

FRENATRACA is a populist group formed in 1962 by the Caceres brothers, local businessmen and political bosses in Juliaca in the southern sierra. While it retains support in its birthplace, FRENATRACA is essentially a throwback from the outdated politics of caciquismo.

Trade Unions

Around 800,000 Peruvian workers (about 12 per cent of the labour force) belong to more than 4,500 officially recognised trade unions, with another 250,000 belonging to unrecognised unions. Most unions are workplace-based and small. However, many of them are grouped into national federations, organised on an industry-wide basis. In turn, many of these are affiliated to national confederations. The national confederations are divided along political lines. Political rivalries also mean that in some industries there are competing national federations. There are four national union confederations in Peru:

Confederacion General de Trabajadores del Peru (CGTP)

The largest and most important confederation, the present CGTP was founded in 1968 and took its name from the first Peruvian national union confederation founded under the influence of Jose Carlos Mariategui in 1929. The CGTP's affiliated membership probably totals 500,000 workers, grouped in more than thirty national federations. A majority of the CGTP's executive are members or sympathisers of the PC-U, and it is affiliated to the Moscow-backed World Federation of Trade Unions. Since 1980 the CGTP has become more open politically. As a result, important unions such as the FNTMMP (the Miners' Federation, with 40,000 members) have rejoined, while others, such as the maoist-led SUTEP teachers' union (with more than 100,000 members) have affilated for the first time. Other important affiliates of the CGTP include the building workers (70,000) and bankworkers (25,000). General Secretary: Valentin Pacho.

Confederacion de Trabajadores del Peru (CTP)

Founded in 1944 by Aprista and communist trade union leaders, the CTP quickly came under APRA's control. Its current membership totals around 110,000. The CTP is affiliated to the International Confederation of Free Trade Unions. Since its heyday in the 1940s and 1950s, the CTP's influence has been reduced as a result of a generally moderate line and internal divisions which reflect conflicts within APRA. However, it retains important affiliates in the transport industry, the docks, and the textile industry. The CTP leadership is currently split between a conservative majority faction, headed by

13

veteran leader Julio Cruzado, and a minority supporting dockers' leader Luis Negreiros.

Confederacion Nacional de Trabajadores (CNT)

A small confederation of Christian Democrat inspiration founded in 1971. It has some 16,000 affiliates, split into two factions.

Confederacion de Trabajadores de la Revolucion Peruana (CTRP)

Founded by the military government in 1974, the CTRP currently has less than 10,000 members. Never large, it lost its strongest affiliates when they broke away to form the independent CTRP-Lima as the military government moved to the right.

In 1981, the CTP, the conservative faction of the CNT, and the CTRP formed a working alliance known as the Frente Democratico Sindical.

Independent Unions

Politically influenced by the new left parties, a number of unions left the CGTP in mid-1970s since they disagreed with the confederation's support for the military government. These unions joined others which had never affiliated to the national confederations. Their current membership totals around 250,000. The leading independent unions are Luz y Fuerza (electricity), oilworkers, CITE (civil servants), printers and brewery workers.

Campesino Confederations

Confederacion Campesina del Peru (CCP)

Formed in 1956, incorporating the Federacion de Yanaconas y Campesinos organised in 1947. The CCP's membership includes campesino communities, cooperatives, and leagues of small peasant proprietors. It covers 18 departmental federations, but its main strength is in the sierra, particularly among campesino communities. The leading political force within the CCP is VR, which displaced the PC-U in the early 1970s as a result of the PC-U's support for the Velasco agrarian reform, which largely neglected the campesino communities. President: Andres Luna Vargas.

Confederacion Nacional Agraria (CNA)

Formed by the Velasco government in 1974, the CNA was denied official backing when it became increasingly critical of the military regime. Most of its affiliates are agricultural cooperatives and Social Interest Agrarian Societies (SAISs) created by the military government's agrarian reform. Its main strength is on the coast. The dominant political force within the CNA is the PSR. General Secretary: Felipe Huaman.

In 1983 both the CCP and the CNA joined a coordinating committee of agricultural organisations known as the Congreso Unitario Nacional Agrario (CUNA). Its other members included the Organizacion Nacional Agraria (small and medium private farmers) and sectoral committees of commercial farmers.

The Armed Forces and Police

The armed forces have played a decisive role in Peru's political history. Since 1930 there have been four periods of military rule lasting for a total of thirty years. For most of this century the military's political interventions were in support of the right, but during the Velasco government (1968-75) a new current of reformist nationalism became dominant within the armed forces. While Velasquismo still retains a presence, military opinion appears to have swung back to the right. Following extensive arms purchases over the last decade, all three services are equipped with modern weapons. During the military government the Soviet Union displaced France and the United States as Peru's main weapons supplier. While recent orders have also included Soviet weapons, the balance in arms purchases has tilted back towards Western Europe and the US. High defence spending is justified by military chiefs on the grounds of long-running border tensions with both Ecuador and Chile. The frontier conflict with Ecuador is the more volatile since Ecuador repudiates the Rio de Janeiro Protocol legalising Peru's annexation of disputed frontier areas in 1941. Small-scale clashes occur almost every year. In 1981 these escalated into a short border war in the Cordillera del Condor. The Peruvian armed forces are also currently engaged in counter-insurgency operations against Sendero Luminoso.

The army has a peacetime strength of 70,000, of whom 49,000 are conscripts. Its weaponry includes 250 Soviet-made T54 and T55 tanks, 170 French and US medium and light tanks, and 42 Soviet M18 helicopters.

The airforce rivals those of Argentina and Brazil as the strongest in Latin America. Its 10,000 troops operate more than 120 combat aircraft, including 24 Mirage fighters, 32 Soviet Sukhoi fighters, US Bell, Soviet M18 and Hind helicopters. The airforce placed an order for 24 advanced Mirage interceptors in 1982.

The 12,000 strong navy is traditionally the most politically conservative of the three forces. Its fleet expansion programme includes the purchase of six new West German submarines, and the construction of two Italian-designed guided-missile frigates at the navy's shipyards at Callao. The fleet also includes 2 cruisers, eight destroyers, six frigates and five submarines. Some of these ships are armed with Exocet missiles.

Peru has three police forces administered by the ministry of the interior. Their total strength is around 45,000. All are armed, although they lack the heavy weaponry of some of their Latin American counterparts. The largest of the forces is the uniformed Guardia Civil (GC), which functions as a general constabulary. The Policia de Investigaciones del Peru (PIP) is a plain clothes detective force. The Guardia Republicana (GR) is a small para-military force which guards the frontiers, prisons and state installations. Both the GC and the GR have specialised counter-insurgency battalions.

All three armed forces and both the GC and the PIP have separate intelligence services. The Servicio de Intelligencia Nacional (SIN) is intended to coordinate their work, but inter-force rivalries have limited its effectiveness. With the rise of Sendero Luminoso's insurgency, the SIN budget has recently been significantly expanded.

2 Colony and Republic

The Inca Empire

When the Spanish conquistadores arrived in the land they called Peru in 1532, it already possessed a human history going back 20,000 years. However, the Inca Empire which the Spanish defeated was of recent origin. During the fifteenth century, the Incas had rapidly conquered a territory covering the length of the Andes and the Pacific coast from northern Ecuador to central Chile. The Incas imposed an efficient state bureaucracy, their version of the Quechua language and worship of the sun on an agricultural society whose traditional structure they changed little. Its basic communal and productive unit was known as the ayllu. Many ayllus had plots of land at differing altitudes, enabling them to grow not only maize, potatoes and indigenous grains, but also coca leaves and hot peppers in the Andean foothills. In the high altitude pastures of the Andean plateaux, ayllus had flocks of llamas and alpacas, producing wool and meat and acting as beasts of burden.

Ayllus were grouped together under local chieftains (kurakas) who generally held larger landholdings of their own. Under a system of labour service known as the mita, members of the ayllu worked the kurakas' lands in return for part of the produce and military protection. In a sophisticated system of labour cooperation, members of different ayllus worked communally on larger tasks, such as the construction and maintenance of extensive irrigation systems. As they conquered, the Incas took over some of the land of kurakas and ayllus alike, but they preserved the paternalistic tradition of handing back part of the produce yielded by the mita. Although they were authoritarian rulers, the Incas ensured that a large population (estimates vary between 12 and 32 million for the empire as a whole), received basic material necessities, an achievement never since equalled in Peruvian history.

In the 1520s, when it was still consolidating the conquest of outlying regions, the empire was weakened by a devastating plague. The Inca ruler, Huayna Kapac, was amongst its victims, and his death triggered a civil war over succession between two of his sons, Atahualpa and Huascar. Atahualpa eventually won, but at the cost of imperial unity. Consequently, when Pizarro and his 180 conquistadores landed in Tumbes in 1532, they faced an enfeebled and divided empire. Enlisting the support of a number of discontented kurakas and holding a decisive advantage in military technology, the Spaniards rapidly conquered the Inca domain. Though scattered resistance continued for some 30 years, the murder of Atahualpa and the sacking of the Inca capital of Cusco broke the empire.

Spanish Colonialism

The Spaniards shattered the ordered, cooperative world of the Andean Indian campesino (peasant farmer). Mining for export to Europe became the dominant activity around which the colonial economy was organised. Peru entered the world economy as an exporter of raw materials and importer of manufactured articles, a role that it has never relinquished. The Spanish crown used silver and gold from Peru to pay for its European wars, and much of this Peruvian wealth ended up in Britain and France, providing an important source of capital for commercial and industrial development.

Unlike the European colonisation of North America, only relatively small numbers of Spaniards settled in Peru. They therefore relied on Indian labour to work the mines. The Spaniards adopted and abused the traditional mita as a means to acquire labourers from the Indian communities. Under the Spaniards the mita ceased to be a cooperative institution which placed obligations on the ruler as well as the labourer. Indian miners worked six or seven days a week in the rich silver mine of Potosi, and at Huancavelica where mercury (used in the smelting of silver) was mined. Since the Spanish had little interest in prolonging the working life of each labourer, the conditions under which the mitayos worked were extremely bad. A great many Indians died in the mines to be replaced by new groups of workers, often uprooted from their settlements by force. The mita and its disruptive effect on traditional agriculture, together with the arrival of European diseases (measles, influenza and smallpox) to which the Indians had no resistance, reduced the Indian population to around two million by 1600.

The Spanish crown took over the lands of the Inca rulers, but in theory the lands of the Indian campesinos were left alone. In practice, the Church and an emerging criollo elite (Americans of Spanish descent) dispossessed the ayllus of much of the best agricultural land on the coast as well as the highland valley pastures near the mines. There they established large estates (haciendas), supplying agricultural produce to the mines and the coastal towns. Sheep wool became an important commercial product, being both exported and woven in local textile mills that were also worked by forced Indian labour. Because the Indian population in many coastal valleys was wiped out by disease, the Spaniards imported increasing numbers of slaves from Africa to work on plantations. In the Andean highlands (sierra) haciendas were established on more feudal lines with Indians receiving plots of estate land in return for their labour.

In the late sixteenth century Viceroy Toldeo grouped together remaining ayllus into compact communities for administrative convenience. As well as providing labour service under the mita these Indian communities had to pay tribute to the Crown in money or specified products, the prices of which were fixed by the Crown. The Indians were also forced to buy artefacts imported from Spain and distributed at inflated prices by royal officials. In this way, the Indian communities were forced into the market economy and provided for the upkeep of the colonial state. Toledo made the kurakas responsible for the collection of tribute and the provision of forced labour. Although some kurakas and a very small caste of descendents from the Inca nobility acquired considerable wealth and adopted a Spanish lifestyle, colonial Peru was essentially divided along ethnic lines. As well as being economically exploited the Indian population was culturally isolated, racially despised, and its traditional religions were attacked by the Catholic church. Periodic rebellions against white domination were normally led by members of the Indian elite, who united both Indians and mestizos (people of mixed Indian and white descent) around the symbolic aim of the restoration of the Inca empire. These rebellions were often very violent and even more violently suppressed, but they were generally localised.

In keeping with the export orientation of the colonial economy, Pizarro had founded his capital Lima on the coast. Cusco and other Andean towns, apart from the mining centres, decayed. For two and a half centuries Lima remained the administrative capital of the whole of Spanish South America and the seat of the Inquisition. All trade between Spain and its South American empire passed through the city which by 1796 had a population of more than 50,000.

With the virtual exhaustion of the Potosi and Huancavelica mines in the eighteenth century, Peru was eclipsed as the centre of economic power in Spanish South American both by Venezuela and the River Plate region, whose exports of agricultural products were increasingly important. Meanwhile, royal revenues and control had been diminished by the growing independence of criollo officials and contraband trade in British and French goods.

In response to these problems, the Spanish Bourbon king Charles III introduced sweeping changes in colonial rule which weakened the economic and political power of Lima. He created separate administrative units based on the River Plate, Chile and Upper Peru (Bolivia). Ecuador, Colombia and Venezuela had previously been removed from Lima's jurisdiction, when the Viceroyalty of New Granada was formed in 1717. Charles III also effectively decreed free trade between America and Europe, ending Lima's monopoly. The main beneficiaries were British and French manufacturers and the merchants of Buenos Aires and Valparaiso, whose competition closed down half of Peru's textile mills.

Political Independence

In 1780 the largest of the Indian rebellions against Spanish rule spread through most of southern Peru. It was led by Jose Gabriel Condorcanqui, a Cusco kuraka who took the name of Tupac Amaru II, evoking the memory of the last Inca ruler to resist Viceroy Toledo. As well as Indians, mestizos and fugitive black slaves, Tupac Amaru was initially supported by some provincial criollos. However, the criollo elite of officials and merchants feared the Indian masses even more than they disliked Spanish rule, and they sided with the Crown. Tupac Amaru had initially demanded merely the reform of abuses in colonial rule, but as rebellion and repression spread, the insurgents' aims became the establishment of an Indian and mestizo republic.

Between November 1780 and March 1781, thousands of Indians were killed as the rebellion was put down. Tupac Amaru was finally captured, tortured, beheaded and quartered in the main square of Cusco, along with his wife and other relatives. In reaction to the rebellion, the Crown declared war on the Indian elite, killing and deporting many of its members, abolishing their privileges, and banning the use of Quechua.

This traumatic race war killed off any hope of a national independence movement involving both Indians and criollos. Consequently Peruvian independence was to result largely from the intervention of outside forces. Inspired by the French and United

States' revolutions, and aided by Britain, the merchant class of the River Plate countries and Venezuela had taken advantage of the dislocation of Spanish rule during the Napoleonic Wars to lead national independence movements. But their military leaders, the Argentine Jose de San Martin and the Venezuelan Simon Bolivar realised that as long as Peru remained a royalist stronghold their own position was insecure.

In 1820, having completed the liberation of Chile, San Martin and the British freelance naval commander Lord Alfred Cochrane landed at Paracas, 100 miles south of Lima, with a force of 4,000 troops. The 23,000-strong royalist army, undermined by internal rivalries, retreated to the Andes. San Martin entered Lima and declared Peru independent on 28 July 1821. He then went north to Guayaquil to meet Bolivar. Between them they decided the immediate political future of Peru. The conservative San Martin, who favoured imposing a European-style constitutional monarchy, bowed to the greater military strength of the republican Bolivar. The latter landed at Callao in 1823, San Martin having retired to Argentina. Bolivar's motley army of 9,000 troops, the majority of them Colombian, commanded by the Venezuelan Antonio Jose de Sucre, decisively defeated the royalist forces at the battles of Junin and Ayacucho in the central Andes in 1824.

Caudillismo

The first thirty years of the Republic were marked by economic stagnation and chronic political instability. Geographically isolated from European markets, and with its mines almost worked out, Peru's exports slumped from an annual average of 13.3 million pesos in the second half of the 1780s to 6.3 million pesos in 1820. The war of independence had laid waste haciendas, ports and roads.

The overthrow of the royalist state and the withdrawal of Bolivar to Colombia in 1826 left a political vacuum. Peru fell apart into warring regional factions. Power was contested by military commanders (caudillos) who had fought the Viceroy and went on to fight each other. Between 1826 and 1865, Peru had 34 presidents, 27 of whom were military officers.

Caudillos formed shifting alliances with regional groupings of the provincial criollo elite of landowners and merchants who had been the firmest supporters of independence. These groups had resented both Spanish interference in their affairs and the privileges of the royalist Lima elite. They ensured that the underlying structure of colonial society with its racial divisions remained undisturbed by political

21

independence. Thus, Bolivar's apparently democratic decree of 1824 granting property rights to individual Indians over communal lands enabled criollos to acquire by purchase, deceit or force the lands of many Indian communities that had hitherto eluded them. Bolivar also distributed state lands among his supporters, extending the hacienda system into which more Indians were incorporated as serfs. San Martin's decrees limiting slavery and abolishing the mita and the tribute system were quickly reversed.

British and French merchants replaced Spain in controlling the new republic's foreign trade, to such a degree that they were invited to draft Peru's trade laws in the 1830s. The most important exports were gold and silver (in much reduced quantities), quinine, and sheep and alpaca wool, exported by British merchant houses based in Arequipa. The wool trade fuelled the political ambitions of the southern criollo landowners, who resented the domination of Lima. In the 1830s they organised a short-lived federation of Peru and Bolivia, of which Arequipa would have become the axis. But the federation was crushed by a Chilean invasion in 1839.

The Guano Boom

Republican Peru was hauled out of its economic backwater by the rise of a lucrative export trade in the dung (guano) of the millions of seabirds which feed on the rich fishing grounds of the Pacific coast. Guano had been used locally as a fertiliser since pre-Inca times, but the development of capital intensive commercial agriculture in Europe in the mid-nineteenth century created a massive international market for it. Following the traditional practice of the Spanish crown, the Peruvian government established a state monopoly over the exploitation of guano. It then sub-contracted the trade to British merchant houses, Myers of Liverpool (1840-49) and then Gibbs of London (1849-60). The guano was extracted by Indian and Chinese labourers under appalling conditions. Their skins were shrivelled and some were blinded by the ammonia fumes that guano contains.

Guano breifly converted the Peruvian economy into the most dynamic in Latin America. But in common with other Peruvian booms based on the intensive exploitation and export of raw materials, it brought few benefits to the mass of the population. Although the Peruvian government received in taxes an average of 60 per cent of the net profits of the guano trade between 1840 and 1880, both the economy and the state's finances were more fragile at the end of the boom than they had been before it started. The bulk of guano revenue was spent on the state bureaucracy, the army, and servicing the government's foreign debt. Guano revenues served as collateral for mounting foreign loans, which were often squandered on the import of luxury consumer goods for the elite, and encouraged Peru's British creditors to press for repayment of previous loans. Almost the first act of Peru's first republican government had been to contract loans totalling £1.8 million, but because of the prostrated state of the economy Peru had defaulted on repayment in 1825. In 1848, following pressure from the British ambassador, President Ramon Castilla agreed to place half the state's annual guano income in the Bank of England to pay Peru's outstanding debt which then stood at £4.5 million. Castilla then raised fresh foreign loans to pay off the government's internal debt, borrowed from local landowners and merchants in the years during and after the war of independence. Many fraudulent claims for repayment were filed, and the result was a huge transfer of capital to the criollo elite at the expense of greater state indebtedness to foreign creditors.

This capital transfer consolidated a new commercial bourgeoisie, based on the coast and particularly in Lima. Members of this new rich group gained control over the guano trade by forcing Castilla to terminate the Gibbs contract. This commercial bourgeoisie established Peru's first locally-owned bank, and its first political party, the liberal Civilistas. They also began to invest in large-scale cultivation of sugar and cotton for export. Facing a labour shortage following Castilla's abolition of slavery, they used the compensation to import 100,000 Chinese labourers who were put to work in similar conditions to their African predecessors. Castilla also abolished the Indian tribute since the state no longer depended on it for income. This, however, had the effect of slowing down the development of the local market economy since the Indians were no longer obliged to sell their produce in order to pay the tribute.

In the last years of the guano boom, the government embarked on a programme of railway construction which was to bankrupt the country. The railways were aimed at linking the mines of the central sierra and the big wool haciendas in the south with coastal ports. Hundreds of Chinese labourers died during the building of two trans-Andean railways, engineered by Henry Meiggs, a North American entrepreneur. The railways were largely responsible for a fourfold increase in Peru's foreign debt between 1868 and 1872, when it stood at £35 million, making Peru the largest debtor in the London money market. This crushing debt burden led to the return to foreign hands of control over the guano trade. In 1870 the government granted a monopoly to the French merchant house of Auguste Dreyfus, linked to the Paris bank Societe General. In return, Dreyfus assumed the service of Peru's foreign debt and provided a cash advance to the government. According to Societe General's director, it was 'the biggest, most positive and most lucrative business deal in the world.'

The War of the Pacific

By the late-1870s the guano boom was coming to an end as the richer deposits were exhausted. Cheaper alternatives, such as the nitrates of the Atacama desert and synthetic fertilisers were being developed. In an attempt to supplement declining guano revenues, civilista President Manuel Pardo nationalised the nitrate deposits in Peru's southernmost department of Tarapaca, which like those in the Bolivian Atacama, were being worked by Chilean and British entrepreneurs. But as the world economy moved into recession, nitrate revenue also declined. Unable to raise further foreign loans, the government turned to issuing unbacked paper money until, in 1879, Peru declared itself bankrupt. The guano bubble had finally burst, gravely weakening the republic at a time when it was threatened by an international scramble for control over the nitrate trade. In the same year as the Peruvian default, the Bolivian congress responded to a similar economic crisis by imposing a tax on nitrate exports. This provided Chile with a pretext to declare war on Bolivia, with whom Peru had a treaty of mutual defence. The war that followed ruthlessly exposed the fragility of the Peruvian state, and the indigenous population's lack of identification with the Peruvian 'nation' of the coastal elite. Peruvian preparedness for war had been undermined by the state's bankruptcy and the disbanding of much of the army by Pardo, an anti-militarist. Despite individual acts of naval and military heroism, the Chileans (who were supplied and financed by Britain) took Lima in 1881, and occupied much of the country. By the time they withdrew in 1884 Lima had been sacked and many coastal haciendas were in ruins. Under the terms of the peace settlement, Chile annexed Tarapaca and Tacna, as well as the Bolivian department of Antofagasta.

Civilian politicians emerged from the war with their prestige reduced. The Civilistas had favoured an early peace, preferring defeat to the war's destruction of property and threat to social order. General Andres Caceres, who had led an effective guerrilla campaign against the Chileans in the sierra, became president, inaugurating a further ten years of caudillismo. His immediate problem was to reconstruct the shattered economy. Faced with an acute shortage of capital, he opened negotiations with Peru's foreign creditors. In an agreement known as the Grace Contract, the creditors agreed to cancel Peru's debt in return for a lease giving them control over the railway system, a 4.5 million acre jungle land grant, the promise of 3 million tons of guano, and 33 annual payments of £80,000.

The Rise of the Agro-Export Oligarchy

For Manuel Gonzalez Prado, a dissident nationalist intellectual, Peru's collapse in the war stemmed from 'the profound division of the nation into gentlemen and serfs . . . Our form of government is reduced to a great lie because a state in which two or three million individuals live outside the law doesn't merit the title of a democratic republic.' But the coastal elite were incapable of healing this division since their control of the country depended on a political alliance with the semi-feudal landlords of the sierra, who were the immediate beneficiaries of serfdom. Instead, the coastal elite saw the solution lying in the exploitation of Peru's rich and varied natural resources. This would create an export economy which would generate a more stable and broadly-based prosperity than the guano boom had done. In was an early version of the 'trickle down' theory of economic development, still favoured by liberal economists. With raw material prices high before and during the First World War, Peru's exports grew rapidly, expanding at an average rate of seven per cent a year from 1890 to 1929. This export boom was based on a range of products that was unusually wide for a Latin American country. Sugar, cotton, wool, rubber, silver, copper and oil were each responsible for more than 15 per cent of total export earnings at different times during this period.

This dynamic export growth brought with it important changes in social and economic structure. It consolidated the political and economic power of the small group of coastal sugar and cotton hacendados, who became known as the oligarchy. It also resulted in a near-total takeover of key sectors of the economy — mining and oil — by foreign companies, most of them from the US. Between them, the oligarchy and foreign capital presided over capitalist development in Peru. The oligarchy, made up of around fifty families, allied with the semi-feudal landowners of the sierra and foreign capital, and exercised effective control over the policy of both civilian and military governments almost uninterrupted until General Velasco took power in 1968.

The sugar hacendados made up the most powerful wing of the oligarchy. Sugar production was centred on large mechanised haciendas in the irrigated valleys of the north coast, run on capitalist lines with a stable force of wage labourers. Most of the labourers were

Chinese or sierra campesinos trapped into debt bondage by labour agents who offered them loans or alcohol. The owners of these large haciendas gained monopoly control over water rights, enabling them to bankrupt small proprietors whose lands they absorbed. A steep fall in sugar prices in the late 1920s ruined many smaller hacendados, with the result that half of all sugar land became concentrated in the hands of a duopoly: the German immigrant Gildemeisters and the Graces, Irish-American immigrants whose Peruvian sugar activities provided a platform for the formation of WR Grace and Company, a US-based chemical and trading multinational. In contrast to the sugar haciendas, cotton estates tended to be divided up among share-cropping tenant farmers, who contracted migrant labourers from the sierra for the peak labour periods of sowing and harvest. Cotton production became concentrated in the northern department of Piura and in Ica, on the coast south of Lima. The processing and export of cotton and its by-products was controlled by foreign merchant houses.

The development of the mines and railways (which were extended to La Oroya and Cusco in the 1890s) resulted in the transformation of some sierra haciendas into commercial sheep and cattle ranching enterprises. However, these did not achieve the same degree of mechanisation nor the capitalist labour relations of the coastal sugar plantations. The majority of sierra haciendas continued to be run on semi-feudal lines, their workers allocated tiny plots of land in return for their otherwise unpaid labour. For the hacienda owners, known as 'gamonales', the land was not so much a source of great wealth but simply of 'power in its crudest form. This they exercised on horseback, with whip and shotgun.' They were the law and the local authority in their areas, the only channel of communication and control between the state and the mass of the still predominantly Quechua-speaking Indian population. In the early years of this century, a new wave of hacienda expansion further reduced the lands of the remaining independent Indian communities, and the arrival of the railways, rather than promoting 'trickle down' regional economic development in the central and southern sierra, stimulated a migrationary wave towards Lima and the coast which reached massive proportions as the century wore on.

Peruvian entrepreneurs had successfully revived the mining industry in the last quarter of the nineteenth century as new deposits were discovered and exploited throughout the sierra. However, the formation in New York in 1901 of the Cerro de Pasco Mining Company by millionaire James B. Haggin presaged a rapid US take-over of the bulk of Peru's expanding and profitable mining sector. The Cerro de Pasco Corporation bought up almost all the mines in the central sierra, then the most important mining region in the country, producing copper, silver, lead and zinc. Northern Peru Mining Company (a subsidiary of the US mining giant ASARCO) took over the multi-ore mines in the northern sierra, while the Vanadium Corporation acquired the world's then largest vanadium deposit. By 1930, these three companies were responsible for all but three per cent of Peru's mineral exports (although part of their share corresponded to ore mined by locally-owned companies and then smelted and exported by Cerro). This colonisation of an industry was not due to the Peruvian companies' inability to develop and run the mines efficiently, but to the US firms' greater wealth, which meant they could make cash offers which the Peruvian owners found difficult to refuse.

The foreign oil companies contributed even less to the local economy than the mining giants. Peru was the most important South American oil producer until surpassed by Venezuela in 1924. Production was centred on the oilfields near Talara in the northern desert. The largest field, the La Brea y Parinas Hacienda, was bought while already in production in 1899 by London and Pacific Petroleum. Standard Oil of New Jersey bought out London and Pacific Petroleum and a local oil-distribution company in 1913. Standard Oil assigned its Peruvian operations to a Canadian-based subsidiary, the International Petroleum Company (IPC), which retained the dominant position in the Peruvian oil industry until the 1960s since when few new sources of oil were found. IPC's repatriation of massive profits and exemption from taxes became a major political issue until the company, already winding down its operations having almost exhausted the field, was finally expropriated in 1968.

Foreign ownership of the oil and mining industries deprived Peru of an important potential source of development capital. Within the space of thirty years foreign penetration of the export economy had become so great that the vice president of Citibank said in 1927 that, 'the vast majority of the principal sources of wealth in Peru . . . are controlled by foreign owners, and apart from wages and taxes, none of the value of production is retained in the country.' With US firms responsible for the bulk of foreign ownership, the US displaced Britain as Peru's major trading partner, ending a century of British commercial domination. By 1926 more than a third of Peruvian exports went to the US, and almost half to its imports were supplied by the US.

3 The Birth of Mass Politics

The years of dynamic export growth coincided with a period of political stability in which Peru was ruled almost uninterrupted by elected civilian governments from 1895 to 1919. But the electorate was small, and during the 'aristocratic republic' governments, with one brief exception, represented oligarchic interests. However, industrial growth in Lima and the emergence of capitalist enterprise in the mines, oilfields and sugar estates had created a small but geographically concentrated working class of wage labourers who began to organise in trade unions. The first unions, strongly influenced by anarcho-syndicalism, were formed by Lima artisans at the turn of the century. The first general strike took place in Lima in 1911, in support of workers at a British-owned textile factory in Vitarte who were demanding the eight hour day. By 1918 the anarcho-sydicalist Federacion Obrera Local de Lima was strong enough to organise another general strike which succeeded in winning the eight hour day for organised workers throughout the capital.

Labour unrest was fuelled by a steep rise in the cost of living, triggered internationally by the First World War and exacerbated locally by Peru's growing dependence on imported food — a result of the displacement of food crops by sugar and cotton. Riots and strikes in protest at price increases brought down the aristocratic republic in 1919. The elected president, Augusto Leguia, used the disorders as a pretext to close congress and impose a civilian dictatorship which, with military support, lasted for the next eleven years. An authoritarian populist and successful businessman, Leguia initially distanced himself from the oligarchy, seeking a political base in the expanding middle class of professionals and public employees. In an effort to defuse social tension, he extended the eight hour day to all wage labourers, and decreed a minimum wage. He also established a government indigenous affairs office and appointed a land commission to investigate campesino grievances following a series of agrarian rebellions in Puno in the early 1920s. Leguia set out to modernise the country's physical infrastructure in a public works programme financed by loans from US banks. Urban transport, water and sewerage systems were improved, and work started on large irrigation projects on the coast. By means of a law requiring every male between the ages of 18 and 60 to give 12 days free labour a year, 1,100 miles of road were built. This programme gave rise to a tenfold increase in Peru's foreign debt, and was accompanied by unprecedented corruption. In a particularly glaring example, Citibank paid US$450,000 to the president's son to clinch a US$50 million loan agreement.

Having consolidated his hold on power, Leguia had turned quickly to repression and an accommodation with oligarchic interests. He sent the army into Puno, deported a number of opposition leaders and settled the dispute over IPC's tax obligations in the company's favour. Leguia's shift to the right was in part a response to the emergence in the 1920s of radical political currents which expressed the first coherent opposition to the domination of Peru by the oligarchy and foreign capital. The birth of these political movements — APRA and the Communist Party — was accompanied by a vigorous intellectual debate about the nature of Peruvian society and revolutionary strategy between two of the most influential political thinkers that Latin America has produced — Jose Carlos Mariategui and Victor Raul Haya de la Torre (see box on page 30).

The populist Peruvian Aprista Party, founded by Haya de la Torre in 1928, rapidly became the first mass political party in Peru, drawing its support from the lower middle class, students, and urban and rural workers, mainly in those areas where capitalism was most developed. In particular, APRA gained a solid and lasting base on the north coast, winning the support of the sugar workers and the local middle class who had been marginalised by the monopolisation of the sugar industry. APRA constructed a leadership cult around the charismatic figure of Haya de la Torre, giving the party as quasi-religious character which was reinforced by the severe repression it suffered.

APRA competed for working class support with the small Peruvian Socialist Party (PSP), founded by Mariategui and a group of intellectuals and trade union leaders in 1928. Under Mariategui's influence, anarcho-syndicalism had lost ground to marxism in the trade union movement during the 1920s. In 1929, at the instigation of the PSP, many of the most important unions came together in a marxist trade union federation — the Confederacion General de Trabajadores del Peru (CGTP). The following year, after the first Latin American Congress of the Comintern, and Mariategui's death,

Mariategui and Haya de la Torre

Jose Carlos Mariategui (1895-1930) was the first thinker to attempt a systematic analysis of Latin American realities from a marxist perspective. A Lima journalist, he became a marxist while in Europe between 1920 and 1923. But he was also influenced by the Peruvian 'indigenista' intellectual movement of the early 1920s. The 'indigenistas' resurrected the study of the pre-conquest heritage, and supported the claims of the Indian population to land and social justice.

Mariategui followed the orthodox view of the theoreticians of the Communist International in seeing Peru as a semi-colonial country. However, the Comintern held that Peru was also a feudal society which required a 'national bourgeois' revolution before capitalism and, at a later stage, socialism could develop. Mariategui, on the other hand, argued that while the landlord class had 'maintained a semi-feudal organisation in agriculture', capitalist development was simultaneously taking place in Peru under the guidance of foreign (British and subsequently US) imperialism. This meant that, 'the landlord class has not succeeded in transforming itself into a capitalist bourgeoisie', but rather 'it has been content to serve as an intermediary for imperialism'.

As a result, the landlord class was incapable of carrying out the task of national economic liberation (the 'national bourgeois revolution' of the Comintern) for which it saw no need. For Mariategui, the middle class was equally incapable of this task because of its racist disdain for, and cultural isolation from, the mass of the Indian population, although the middle class's 'own mixed blood is all too evident'. Furthermore, Mariategui argued that in the era of monopoly capitalism on a world scale it was too late for autonomous capitalist development to take place in semi-colonial countries. A bourgeois revolution in Peru was therefore doomed to fail.

Consequently, for Mariategui socialism was the only viable form that an anti-imperialist revolution could take: 'This is a moment when it is not possible to be effectively nationalist and revolutionary without being socialist'. However, Mariategui believed that the small size and short history of the Peruvian industrial working class meant that the establishment of a traditional Marxist-Leninist vanguard party was premature. He also argued that the campesinos constituted an important anti-capitalist class because of their struggle for land and their traditional collectivist organisation. But winning campesino support required the formation of a worker-peasant alliance — a conception of party organisation very distinct from the 'purely proletarian party' favoured by the Comintern, then in its most sectarian phase.

Mortally ill, and under intense pressure from the Comintern to combat Haya de la Torre's populist nationalism Mariategui lost the debate on party organisation and failed to construct a marxist movement adapted to the specific realities of Peruvian society. Yet he bequeathed a powerful intellectual legacy, which more than fifty years later is claimed by most of the major forces on the Peruvian left.

Victor Raul Haya de la Torre (1895-1979), from Trujillo on the sugar-growing north coast, began his political career as a student leader in Lima during the 1919 general strike. Deported by Leguia, he founded the Alianza Popular Revolucionaria Americana (APRA) as an anti-imperialist movement on a continental scale. Its five founding principles were: the struggle against 'Yankee imperialism'; the political unity of Latin America; the nationalisation of land and industry; the internationalisation of the Panama Canal; and solidarity with all oppressed peoples and classes of the world. Haya was inspired by the Mexican revolution and the Chinese Kuo-Mintang rather than communism, which he rejected as alien to the specific realities of Indoamerica (as he called Latin America).

For Haya, Indoamerica's problem lay in the alliance between foreign capital and domestic feudalism. However, he held that imperialism in Indoamerica was the first rather than the last stage of capitalism, arguing that a national anti-imperialist revolution which would organise national capitalist development was both necessary and viable. In this he assigned a key role to the rapidly growing middle class. By directing his appeal to this social group, Haya was able to create a mass political party in Peru much more successfully than the pro-Moscow leaders of the Communist Party, who concentrated their efforts on the small industrial proletariat. But APRA's socially heterogenous base and its diffuse ideology provided few defences against the opportunism to which the party quickly fell victim.

the PSP changed its name to the Peruvian Communist Party (PCP) and affiliated to the Third International. Under the leadership of Eudocio Ravines and at the behest of the Comintern, the PCP adopted sectarian positions which impeded it from winning mass support.

The Military Defends the Oligarchy

The onset of the Great Depression exposed Peru's acute dependence on the US economy converting a stagnation in the Peruvian economy which had begun in the late 1920s into a major crisis. Total export earnings fell by more than two thirds between 1929 and 1932, the flow of fresh bank loans from the US ceased and Peru defaulted on its foreign debt repayments. Mining and sugar enterprises laid off half their workforce, while the cotton estates suspended the hiring of 40,000 migrant labourers. Workers who retained their jobs faced wage cuts.

In August 1930 Luis Sanchez Cerro, a mestizo army commander, overthrew Leguia and proceeded to repress workers' demonstrations while seeking popular support with food distribution programmes. Ravines and the Communist Party argued that a revolutionary situation existed, and attempted to establish soviets and seize power. This policy was to end in bloody failure, above all in the Cerro Corporation mines of the central sierra. Faced with sackings and wage cuts, the Cerro miners staged an insurrection which shook the US embassy sufficiently for it to request the sending of US marines. But on November 8 1930, when miners' leaders were assembled in La Oroya to discuss affiliation to the CGTP, the police swooped and arrested them all. In a subsequent demonstration by miners and construction workers near La Oroya, 23 workers were killed by the police. A strike and demonstrations by workers at the IPC oilfields ended with further killings and arrests. The miners and oilworkers unions were dismantled, the CGTP and the Communist Party were banned and their leaders arrested or driven underground. The CGTP effectively ceased to exist, while the PCP embarked on a lengthy period of clandestinity in which it became isolated from what remained of the trade union movement.

Sanchez Cerro was forced to step down in March 1931 owing to rivalries within the armed forces. He was replaced by a junta which called elections under a broadened franchise giving the vote to all literate adult males (or one adult in five). Haya de la Torre was permitted to return from exile and the main contenders in the elections were APRA and Sanchez Cerro's fascist-like Union Revolucionaria. Haya toned down APRA's previous revolutionary position, issuing a minimum programme whose main points were an expanded state role in the economy, protection for locally-owned industry, social reform, and measures to control the 'excesses' of foreign investment. The US ambassador cabled to Washington: 'I am able to believe that if (Haya) should become president of Peru we would have nothing to fear.' It was the beginning of APRA's long march to the right.

The oligarchy, however, was not as sanguine. In a result which APRA denounced as fraudulent, Sanchez Cerro gained 51 per cent of the vote, and Haya 35 per cent. Blocked from assuming power by peaceful means, Aprista activists rose in Trujillo in July 1932. They held the city for two days, killing some 60 army officers they had captured. When the army re-took Trujillo they rounded up more than a thousand suspected Apristas and shot them at the pre-Inca ruins of Chan Chan outside the city. The division of the radical and labour movement between the divergent currents of Aprismo and communism had quickly proved to have tragic consequences from which the oligarchy was to continue to profit. The Trujillo uprising and its bloody aftermath sparked a feud between the army and APRA which was to last for almost half a century. It was fuelled by repeated Aprista attempts to infiltrate the lower ranks of the army during the 1930s. This feud resulted in a military veto on the entry of APRA into government, and drove the party into clandestinity. For all the incoherence of its policies, APRA was the only popularly-backed alternative to oligarchic rule, and its isolation contributed to the political stagnation of the following decades.

Sanchez Cerro (assassinated by an Aprista) was succeeded by Oscar Benavides (president 1933-39), a hard-line general of fascist tendencies. Benavides combined strict economic orthodoxy and political repression with paternalistic measures of limited social reform, designed to woo the middle class from Aprismo.

Missed Opportunities

Having eliminated the immediate threat posed by APRA and the PCP with repression, the military felt able to call elections in 1939. APRA and the PCP were both banned from standing, but gave their support to Manuel Prado, who won comfortably. A Lima banker, Prado (1939-45), like Leguia before him, initially sought a political base in the middle class by taking some timid anti-oligarchic steps. Aprista and communist union leaders were allowed to form a new national trade union federation, the Confederacion de Trabajadores del Peru (CTP), which rapidly came under Aprista control. An interlude of political harmony based on modest export growth was strengthened by a brief and successful border war with Ecuador provoked by the international oil companies. The war resulted in Peru confirming its hold over an extensive tract of disputed jungle territory, later found to be oil-bearing.

Prado was succeeded by Jose Luis Bustamante y Rivero (1945-48), heading the National Democratic Front whose major member was APRA. His election was accompanied by large popular mobilisations and demands for radical change. But APRA's main concern was to maintain its newly-won legality. According to Haya, APRA would not 'take wealth from those who have it but to create it for those who don't'. Impressed by Roosevelt's New Deal, Haya had also reversed his position on US imperialism, calling for a 'democratic inter-americanism without empires', a formula which masked the end of Aprista opposition to foreign investment. The Bustamante government failed to implement a coherent alternative economic policy, but in an effort to satisfy its political base, the government increased wages, controlled prices and imposed exchange controls. Thus, against a background of rising inflation and administrative chaos, the oligarchy and its mouthpiece, the Gildermeister-owned newspaper *La Prensa*, campaigned for military intervention. After an Aprista rising by sailors in Callao had been easily suppressed General Manuel Odria staged a coup which restored open oligarchic rule.

Odria (1948-56) imposed an authoritarian dictatorship in which APRA, the trade unions and the PCP again faced repression. Aprista militants were hunted and shot while Haya took refuge in the Colombian Embassy, where he was forced to remain for eight years. The general initiated what economic historians Thorp and Bertram have called 'a remarkable twenty year period of total integration into the international system with complete commitment to the rules of the game'. US President Eisenhower apparently shared this view, since he decorated Odria for his contribution to 'the free enterprise system'. Odria scrapped exchange and price controls, devalued the sol, and gave companies generous tax concessions.

Under the impact of these measures, and with world prices high during the long post-war boom, Peruvian exports grew by around 10 per cent a year during the 1950s, and then doubled this high growth rate in the early 1960s'. Minerals and fish products led the renewed export boom. Odria awarded the iron ore deposits at Marcona to a US company after the state had invested US$2 million in the development of the mine. Only US$8 million more was required to begin production, of which US$4 million was recoverable from the first year's output. The large open-cast copper mine at Toquepala was brought into production by Southern Peru Copper Corporation (SPCC). Thorp and Bertram estimate that only 21 per cent of the income generated by Toquepala in its first six years of production stayed in the country. In part this was because SPCC reported profits of US$135 million to the US government in this period, while to the Peruvian government it reported US$69 million. In contrast to mining, the other major export growth sector, fishing, was largely locally controlled. It was middle class entrepreneurs, rather than the oligarchy or foreign firms, who made fortunes in the fishing industry. The fishing boom was triggered by the adoption of fishmeal as an animal feed in the northern hemisphere during the 1950s. The cold waters of the Humboldt current brought huge shoals of anchovies to the Peruvian coast, and by 1963 154 factories were grinding them into fishmeal. The Peruvian fishing industry became the largest in the world, and the shantytown city of Chimbote on the north coast the world's largest fishing port.

Cracks in the Social Order

The Peruvian economy underwent a major structural change in the 1950s and early 1960s as foreign capital began to invest heavily in manufacturing industry. This industrialisation was accompanied by important social and political changes. New economic groups emerged whose interests were not always compatible with the prevailing export model, while the economic and political position of the weakest link in the oligarchy's coalition — the sierra gamonales — was seriously undermined.

Some growth in the manufacturing sector derived from the processing for local consumption and export of products that had previously been exported as raw materials, such as the manufacture of paper and chemicals from sugar by WR Grace and Company. But the bulk of the new industrial activity involved local production of goods that had previously been imported. The Cerro de Pasco Corporation, for example, began to manufacture locally material required for its mines. However, much of the industrial growth involved foreign companies new to Peru, producing consumer durables (cars and fridges) and industrial inputs (cement and rubber). Peruvian entrepreneurs also began to invest in industry, although this was often as junior partners in joint ventures where 'US capital provided the know-how, and Peruvian capital the know-whom', as sociologist Julio Cotler has written. The result was that manufacturing output grew by almost eight per cent a year between 1950 and 1967, a third as fast again as the economy as a whole, so that by 1968 manufacturing accounted for 20 per cent of GDP compared with 14 per cent in 1950. Yet many of the manufacturing plants that were set up were little more than packaging operations for imported products; virtually all were reliant on imported technology and machinery, and thus generated few local spin-offs. While the expansion of employment opportunities was an overriding social priority, the highly mechanised character of these plants meant that manufacturing jobs only doubled between 1950 and 1975 while manufacturing output increased sixfold.

The complete lack of industrial planning meant that the vast majority of the new plants were located in Lima or other coastal cities, accentuating the geographical distortion of the economy. This acted

Land Distribution in Peru in 1961

Type of Farm	Units Numbers	%	Area Total Area (Thousands of hectares[1])	%	Average Unit Area (hectares[1])
Haciendas	10,462	1.2	13,995	52.3	1,338.1
Capitalist farms and small haciendas	23,250	2.7	1,006	3.7	43.3
Family units:					
self-sufficient[2]	98,370	11.5	876	3.3	8.9
'minifundios'[3]	719,110	84.3	1,124	4.2	1.6
Communal lands[4]	2,338	0.3	9,770	36.5	4,179.1
TOTAL	853,530	100.0	26,771	100.0	31.0

Notes:
1. One hectare = 2.47 acres.
2. A 'self-sufficient' family unit is defined as a farm capable of supporting a family.
3. 'Minifundios' are farms which are incapable of supporting a family — they include both parcels of land located within haciendas and individual plots within campesino communities.
4. Communal lands were almost entirely high altitude rough pasture.

Source:
Matos Mar and Mejia: *La Reforma Agraria en el Peru.*

as a powerful magnet for the rural population which was expanding but still continued to be denied access to land by the gamonal system in the sierra. The improvement in transport links and rural education also contributed to the tidal wave of migration to the coast. While the total population more than doubled between 1940 and 1970, greater Lima grew sixfold until, by 1972, more than three million people (or one Peruvian in four) lived in the capital. Huge shanty towns sprang up overnight on the desert fringes of Lima and other coastal cities. Only a minority of those who migrated found permanent work, the remainder forming a growing army of street vendors, domestic servants and casual workers. This impoverished mass of urban settlers ringed the exclusive residential districts of the elite, posing new problems of social control, and placing new demands on a state which had traditionally neglected basic social welfare functions.

Meanwhile, in the sierra the slow spread of modernisation combined with acute land hunger to place the gamonal system under increasing strain. As campesino family plots were further and further sub-divided over generations, Peru came to have the most unequal landholding structure in a continent characterised by extreme inequalities in landownership (see table). While the oligarchy continued to block land reform proposals the campesinos gradually became more organised. APRA began to set up unions of tenant farmers in the 1930s, and in 1947 the Confederacion Campesina del Peru (CCP) was formed, its members including tenants, small proprietors and campesino communities. This organisational progress manifested itself in a wave of campesino militancy which flared across the sierra in the 1950s and early 1960s. Strikes and rent strikes by hacienda workers and tenants, and mass invasions of hacienda lands by neighbouring communities and landless labourers combined in a massive movement to recover ancestral lands from the gamonales. The invasions were normally met by police repression, which prompted a radical response in the coffee growing valleys of La Convencion and Lares in the high jungle near Cusco. Encouraged by Hugo Blanco, a Quechua-speaking trotskyist and former student leader, leagues of small tenant farmers staged a year-long strike and land occupation, and began to arm themselves against the police. The protests in the sierra forced the second Prado government (1956-62) to establish an agrarian reform commission, but after four years of deliberation no concrete proposals had been made.

Belaunde and Accion Popular

The professional and middle class grew rapidly under the impact of industrialisation and urbanisation with white collar employment doubling during the 1950s to total 15 per cent of the workforce. This expanding middle class provided the social base for two new political movements which offered a moderate challenge to the oligarchy's rule. Accion Popular (AP) and the Christian Democratic Party (PDC) both originated in Arequipa, a regional centre of opposition to the Odria dictatorship, and a city with an unusually dynamic provincial bourgeoisie. Both parties were committed to the modernisation and development of Peru through social and economic reform within the framework of parliamentary democracy. They favoured limited state intervention in the economy, in the context of a technocratic development model involving national planning, industrialisation and an agrarian reform aimed at increasing the efficiency of Peruvian agriculture. Accion Popular, in particular, emphasised an expansion of state educational provision and public works programmes. The party's founder, Fernando Belaunde Terry, an Arequipa architect trained at the University of Texas, expressed a vague nationalism in his slogan 'Peru as a doctrine' and in appeals to indigenous traditions of popular cooperation in order to develop the country's infrastructure and physical resources. Belaunde emerged as a charismatic political force in the 1956 election campaign, when he toured the normally politically neglected sierra promising land reform. But the elections, in which literate women were allowed to vote for the first time, were won by the conservative Manuel Prado, who received the backing of APRA in return for a promise to lift Odria's ban on the party. It was the beginning of an open alliance between APRA and the oligarchy which lasted for the next twelve years.

The contest between Belaunde and APRA reached deadlock in the 1962 elections, with Haya receiving 33 per cent of the vote and Belaunde 32.1 per cent. Amidst allegations of fraud, and after Haya had struck a deal with Odria, the army stepped in to prevent APRA coming to power. The junta (1962-63) provided the first evidence of a growing current of nationalist reform within the armed forces. The junta founded the National Planning Institute and built a state-owned oil refinery near Lima. It also enacted a limited land reform decree, suspending the labour obligations of tenants in La Convencion and Lares, enabling them to buy their plots. However, at the same time more than a thousand left-wing and campesino leaders were rounded up, Hugo Blanco being imprisoned in the offshore 'Devil's Island' prison of El Fronton.

The military called fresh elections in June 1963 in which Belaunde, this time in alliance with the PDC, won 36.3 per cent against Haya's 34.4 per cent. But the opposition Aprista-Odrista alliance controlled congress, and blocked many of Balaunde' policy initiatives. Eschewing mass mobilisation as a counterweight to oligarchic opposition, the Belaunde government rapidly lost the reformist impetus of the campaign trail and acquired an increasingly technocratic character. On the key issue of land reform, it introduced legislation of limited scope which was further watered down by congress. Under its provisions, less than 15,000 families received land between 1964 and 1969. Most of these land transfers simply regulated previous land invasions, the beneficiaries having to purchase land they considered to be their own. In place of a radical land re-distribution, Belaunde put greater emphasis on the colonisation of the high jungle to 'extend the agricultural frontier', increase food production, and defuse campesino militancy in the sierra. The colonisation scheme was linked to a grandiose project to build a highway running the length of the country along the jungle fringe, with which Belaunde developed a particular personal obsession. The highway formed part of an expanded public investment programme financed by foreign loans, and centred on transport and irrigation projects, and improvements in the educational system.

This programme embodied much of the spirit of US President John Kennedy's Alliance for Progress, launched to promote moderate reform throughout Latin America as a defence against the spreading of radical movements in the wake of the Cuban Revolution. Nevertheless, the State Department, which had backed APRA since the 1950s, distrusted Belaunde for his rhetoric over the still unresolved issue of IPC's future, and because the PCP and other left-wing forces had supported the president in the 1963 elections. Once elected, Belaunde was quick to distance himself from the left, but continuing US hostility impeded Peru's access to international development funds.

By the 1960s the rapid expansion of higher education had strengthened the left, which recruited many first generation provincial university students faced with limited career opportunities and shorn of social status by the cultural prejudices of the Lima elite. At the same time APRA's open conservatism and splits in the world communist movement threw up a clutch of new revolutionary parties. Following the Sino-Soviet schism, the PCP divided, with the bulk of the youth section and some regional committees (including that in Ayacucho) forming the maoist PCP Bandera Roja. Bandera Roja then itself split, the bulk of its members forming the Partido Communista del Peru Patria Roja, which followed the Chinese line, while Bandera Roja aligned itself with the Albanian regime. A third group, based in Ayacucho, formed the PC del P Sendero Luminoso (Shining Path), which espoused a fundamentalist maoism.

Meanwhile, the Cuban revolution inspired APRA's left-wing, led by Trujillo lawyer Luis De la Puente Uceda, to leave the party in 1959 to form APRA Rebelde, which subsequently changed its name to the Movimiento de la Izquierda Revolucionara (MIR). The MIR adopted Che Guevara's foquista strategy of rural guerrilla warfare, arguing that small armed groups of revolutionaries could gain the support of the oppressed campesinos of the sierra and initiate a Cuban-style revolutionary war. Two focos were established in 1965, the first on the Andean foothills and high jungle of Junin, and the second under the command of De la Puente near the La Convencion valley in Cusco. The Junin group staged several successful raids on haciendas and police posts. But the MIR had disastrously underestimated its political isolation both from the rest of the left and, more crucially, from the campesinos. An attempt to reach agreement with Hugo Blanco and his supporters in La Convencion failed, while the PCP, which retained the most significant working-class base on the left, criticised guerrilla action as 'adventurist'. The MIR guerrilla groups were mainly composed of middle-class students or professionals from Lima, who could not speak Quechua and who had little experience of conditions in the sierra. In the absence of previous political work, it was illusory for them to expect spontaneous campesino support for their armed struggle. Belaunde ordered the armed forces to eliminate the guerrillas. Supplied with napalm and counter-insurgency advice by the US, the armed forces had little difficulty in wiping out the focos in a matter of months, killing De la Puente and other MIR leaders. Survivors of the guerrilla campaign claimed that several thousand campesino were also killed, but the army reported that only hundreds had died.

In the wake of the guerrilla episode, the later years of the Belaunde government were marked by increased repression, corruption scandals, mounting economic problems and political crisis. In 1967, facing a serious balance of payments problem as the long export boom drew to an end and food imports and foreign debt repayments continued to rise, Belaunde devalued the sol, food prices increased and the government continued to move to the right. As a result, the ruling coalition split, and the Christian Democrats went into opposition. However, the party's right wing, headed by Lima mayor Luis Bedoya Reyes, remained loyal to Belaunde and formed the Partido Popular Cristiano (PPC).

The issue which finally precipitated the fall of the Belaunde government was its mishandling of the controversial oil question. On taking office, Belaunde had pledged to deal with IPC 'in ninety days'. However, the agreement which was finally signed in 1968 was highly favourable to the company. IPC ceded control over the almost exhausted La Brea y Parinas oilfield to the small state oil company EPF, but retained its refinery and its monopoly over petrol marketing in Peru. The contract contained a crucial and secret eleventh page fixing the price at which EPF would sell oil to IPC, guaranteeing the latter healthy profits. The existence of 'Page Eleven' was eventually revealed by EPF's president, setting off a national scandal which divided Accion Popular.

With the government in disarray, the armed forces headed by army commander General Juan Velasco Alvarado staged a bloodless coup. In the early hours of 3 October 1968 tanks surrounded the presidential palace in the heart of Lima. Belaunde was evicted in his pyjamas, and later that day despatched to Buenos Aires. Belaunde's capitulation to IPC dramatised the failure of his government to overcome the structural impediments to Peruvian development posed by the continuing domination of the most productive areas of the economy by foreign capital and the domestic oligarchy. With Belaunde's failure opening the way to a seemingly inevitable Aprista victory in the 1969 elections, the military veto had once again been exercised to prevent Haya from taking power. However, in a more or less conscious attempt to purge the country of Aprismo, Velasco proceeded to implement the main elements in APRA's 1931 Minimum Programme, which Haya himself had long since abandoned.

4 Military Reformism

The Velasco government (1968-1975) implemented a radical programme which marked the first decisive break with the economic model imposed by the Spanish conquest. This involved ending the political domination and economic power of the oligarchy; the modernising of the Peruvian state and a major expansion of its role in the economy; the search for a more equitable relationship with foreign capital and major changes in land and property ownership.

The implementation of this programme by a military regime marked a sharp break in the pattern of Peruvian and Latin American politics, in which the armed forces had traditionally intervened to protect the status quo. This break with orthodoxy reflected both changes inside the Peruvian military and the depth of the problems created by the failure of civilian political forces to modernise Peruvian society. This failure threatened to choke further capitalist development and was, in the view of the military, creating the conditions for a socialist revolution. Far from promoting integrated development through a 'trickle down' process, the growth of the corporate export economy had underlined and accentuated the inequalities in Peruvian society. Income distribution in Peru was amongst the most unequal anywhere in the world, and was becoming more so. The reversal of these inequalities required land reform (to increase both rural incomes and food production), and exchange rate and tariff policies favourable to industrial growth (to provide jobs for the urban unemployed, and reduce dependence on imports). In addition, while Peru's need for foreign exchange to pay its foreign debt and to finance rising food imports had increased, the export economy was in decline. Peru had exhausted its easily exploitable natural resources. The fishing industry was collapsing from overfishing and climatic disturbances. Further growth in agricultural exports required heavy investment in irrigation projects involving the costly diversion of Atlantic-flowing rivers to the Pacific coast; and in the absence of new oil discoveries, Peru had ceased to be an oil exporter. After a century of export diversity, the country was dangerously dependent on minerals (especially copper), but no new mineral projects were being developed by the oligarchy or foreign capital.

The army itself was changing. Officers had traditionally been drawn from the provincial lower middle class, lacking the racial exclusiveness and some of the elitist attitudes of the other services. They had gained first-hand experience of conditions in the sierra during the guerrilla campaign and as a result of military involvement in Belaunde's civic action programmes. The guerrilla episode in particular had served to convince important sections of the army that the continuing division of Peru into two nations was highly threatening to 'national security'. Through the establishment of the Centro de Altos Estudios Militares (CAEM) and a military intelligence service in the 1950s, the army came into contact with intellectual currents that offered a nationalist critique of underdevelopment. Such views, propounded among others by the United Nations Economic Commission for Latin America, were simultaneously gaining ground within the Church and the Peruvian intelligentsia, and provided the theoretical base for a non-communist anti-oligarchic programme. Under these influences, many younger officers, particularly in the army, had come to espouse a new nationalism, which displaced the traditional military subservience to the oligarchy's interests, increasingly identified as anti-national or pro-imperialist.

A charismatic mestizo from a provincial lower middle class background, Velasco himself embodied many of these changed military attitudes. He had relied on a group of young progressive army colonels in planning the 1968 coup. However, he distributed government posts roughly according to military seniority across the three armed services. This initially gave an institutional character to the government, making it an expression of the armed forces as a whole rather than Velasco's personal instrument. It also gave political diversity to a regime in which progressives and conservatives within the armed forces battled for ascendancy, a diversity reflected in the internally contradictory tone of the government's first manifesto. But Velasco's prestige within the armed forces, and the institution's respect for hierarchical structures made him the final arbiter and articulator of policy in a regime which became increasingly autocratic and personalistic. The political process became partly a struggle for Velasco's ear and assent, in which those with privileged access to the president acquired formidable power. Velasco's establishment of a presidential advisory council (COAP), a think tank staffed by many of the young colonels who had planned the coup, gave the progressive elements in the armed forces an important advantage which was subsequently translated into cabinet appointments and key troop commands. With Velasco's backing, the progressives were generally in ascendency between 1969 and 1974. But each major policy initiative was the subject of often bitter internal conflict. This meant that policy-making proceeded by fits and starts, exacerbated by the parade ground style of the regime. Once enacted, policy initiatives were often subject to subsequent revisions in implementation, as individual ministers applied their own stamp to the 'revolutionary process'. While progressive and conservative camps of officers were fairly clearly defined, a large middle group followed a pragmatic line, which shifted both according to specific issues and with the passage of time.

State Capitalism

Velasco's first, symbolic, act was to order troops to occupy and expropriate the IPC refinery at Talara. The government initially refused to pay compensation on the grounds that IPC's tenure was illegal and that the company owed the country the excessive profits it had extracted. The refinery and IPC's monopoly network of petrol stations were turned over to the state oil company, reorganised as Petroperu. The expropriation was greeted with universal acclaim: 'we removed the Esso sign from the country', was how one of Valasco's advisers described it. The IPC expropriation proved to be the first step in a series of nationalisations and state take-overs between 1968 and 1976 that transferred to state ownership the majority of large foreign or oligarchic enterprises in strategic sectors of the economy. The breadth of the nationalisations reflected the new peak in foreign ownership of the economy reached under Belaunde: three-quarters of mining, half of manufacturing industry, two-thirds of the commercial banking system and a third of the fishing industry was under direct foreign control in 1968. On the other hand, the Peruvian state was underdeveloped to a degree unusual even for Latin America. While Belaunde had expanded education and health services, state-owned industry comprised little more than a small steelworks in Chimbote and an oil refinery. Until 1964 the government had not even collected its own taxes, preferring to franchise this to a private company.

The Velasco government nationalised most of the major foreign-owned firms in mining, agro-industry, fishing, banking, electricity supply and transport and communications. These included the Cerro de Pasco Corporation and Marcona Mining Company (from which were created Centromin and Hierroperu respectively). All mineral deposits not being exploited were assigned to a new state mining development corporation, Mineroperu. Also nationalised were the Continental and Internacional banks (majority-owned by the Chase Manhattan and New York Chemical Bank respectively); the Peruvian Corporation, which had retained control over the railway system since the Grace Contract; the Swedish-owned electricity company; the ITT-owned telephone company; and the agricultural and agro-industrial holdings of WR Grace and Company. In parallel moves, the state took over the bankrupt Prado empire (comprising the Banco Popular, and fishing, textile and chemical companies) and the whole of the equally bankrupt fishing sector. New state enterprises were formed to run the ports, airports and parts of Lima's public transport system. A state airline (Aeroperu) and shipping line were established. State companies were granted a monopoly in the marketing of agricultural produce and in the provision of agricultural supplies. By 1975 state enterprises were responsible for more than half of mining output, two-thirds of the banking system, a fifth of industrial production and 50 per cent of total productive investment. The state's share of total production doubled under Velasco to reach 21 per cent in 1975. Its share of exports rose from zero to almost 95 per cent between 1955 and 1975, although an important part of these exports corresponded to minerals and oil marketed but not produced by the state.

In many cases the government paid handsome compensation. In the most notorious example, Chase Manhatten received US$6.3 million for its stake in the Banco Continental, for which it had paid US$1.7 million six years earlier. Chase received 568 soles per share when the market value was 102 soles. The IPC expropriation had prompted the Nixon administration to promote an embargo on credits to the Velasco government from the World Bank and US commercial banks. As a result of this pressure, Peru paid a lump sum of US$76 million to the US government, which then distributed the money among expropriated US companies. Despite the scale of the nationalisations, the government's attitude to foreign capital was pragmatic. Many of the companies taken over were in decline, while some of the mining nationalisations were due to foreign companies' reluctance to make new investments rather than government hostility to foreign capital. SPCC, the newest and most profitable of the foreign mining companies, was not nationalised, in part because it agreed to develop the US$550 million Cuajone copper mine, the only major source of fresh export earnings on the immediate horizon. The government was also pragmatic in signing exploration and service contracts with the US oil companies Occidental and Belco. The companies incurred exploration and development costs in return for half of oil output, the other half going to Petroperu. In both mining and oil, however, all production was marketed by the state. Foreign capital retained a large stake in manufacturing industry. But the more than 200 foreign companies remaining in Peru were legally required to 'Peruvianise' by gradually reducing foreign shareholdings to 49 per cent, and restrictions were placed on profit remittances abroad. However, these rules were frequently waived as the government became increasingly concerned to attract further foreign investment.

The nationalisations were an important element of an integrated development strategy. The plan envisaged a mixed economy, in which state enterprise would co-exist with a 'reformed' private sector, a Yugoslav-style 'socially-owned' sector, and small private businesses. The 'social property' sector of state-sponsored workers' cooperatives was intended to become the predominant form of industrial enterprise. In practice, however, the sector never received adequate financing or promotion, and no more than fifty co-ops were set up. In many cases, these were formed out of bankrupt private companies and inherited their problems. A General Law of Industry established a new legal framework for the private sector, involving the introduction of 'labour communities' in all manufacturing firms with more than five workers (later revised to twenty), as well as in mining, fishing and telecommunications companies. The labour community was a vehicle for workers' participation in management and profits, the law envisaging that by means of annual share distributions the workers would eventually acquire a fifty per cent shareholding in their company. A central role was assigned in the development strategy to further industrialisation, intended to complete the import substitution of the 1950s. The Velasco government stressed state investment in heavy industry: cement, steel, paper, chemicals, glass and shipbuilding were designated the exclusive preserve of the state. At the same time, private manufacturing companies were favoured by increased tariffs and the prohibition of competitive imports, cheap credit from state development banks, cheap industrial inputs from the state sector, and tax incentives to invest. Demand for manufactured goods rose as a result of the government's efforts to distribute income and restrict imports. The participation of Peru in the newly-formed Andean Pact common market was also intended by the government to expand the market for Peruvian industrial products. The Pact, which included Bolivia, Colombia, Ecuador, Venezuela and (until 1976) Chile, established a common external tariff and common rules on foreign investment.

Industrialists were divided in their attitude to the military regime. Larger modern firms, geared towards the export of manufactured goods, and organised in the Exporters' Committee of the Industrialists Society (SNI), tended to cooperate with the government.

More traditional companies, producing for the local market, became increasingly hostile to Velasco, primarily because of the introduction of the labour community and the government's generally conciliatory attitude to the trade unions. Many firms went to great lengths to sabotage the operation of the labour community (such as conducting board meetings in English so that the workers' delegates could not understand the proceedings).

The industrialists also opposed a new labour stability law which gave workers job security after they had completed three months' service, making it much easier for workers to organise. Their political opposition to the government meant that new capital investment by private industrialists fell sharply, although profits rose as manufacturers expanded production by using idle plant to meet increased demand.

Agrarian Reform

The military and their civilian advisers saw land reform not only as a means to neutralise peasant insurgency but also as a key to expanding agricultural production (particularly in the sierra), increasing rural employment, improving income distribution, and thus expanding the rural market for manufactured goods. However, these aims proved both contradictory and impossible to square with the high degree of state control over agriculture which the government imposed. The single most important feature of the Velasco government's thorough-going agrarian reform was that it abolished the economic base of the agro-export oligarchy and the sierra gamonales. The 1969 agrarian reform law declared that all irrigated coastal agricultural landholdings of more than 150 hectares and sierra landholdings of more than 65 hectares, were to be expropriated by the state. Following pressure, both from campesino organisations in the sierra and particularly from rural workers unions on the coast, these limits were subsequently revised downwards to 50 hectares (coast) and 30 hectares (sierra).

The first targets of the agrarian reform were the coastal sugar estates of the Gildemeisters and WR Grace and Company, reflecting both the priority which continued to be given to export agriculture and the symbolic value of moving against the oligarchy's most advanced and efficient holdings. The sugar estates, along with all the other coastal haciendas, were assigned by the state to cooperatives made up of the permanently employed workforce. In the sierra, the reform faced the complex problem of conflicting claims to hacienda lands from landless estate labourers, the hacienda tenants (who in some cases had long since become independent farmers, paying their rent in cash), and the neighbouring campesino communities whose lands had been taken from them by the gamonales over the centuries. The solution adopted was the SAIS, or Social Interest Agrarian Enterprise. Under the SAIS structure, production cooperatives that grouped together the permanent estate labourers farmed the hacienda lands. The surrounding campesino communities with claims to the hacienda lands became associate members of the SAIS. They did not receive land, but instead were to receive a share of the profits of the enterprise and technical advice and services. Former tenants of sierra haciendas were awarded the ownership of the land they previously rented. Many of the SAISs were formed by grouping together several neighbouring haciendas into extensive estates. The reform legislation required those who received land to pay for it, although the price fixed by the government was very low. Exproporiated landowners received most of their compensation in the form of bonds, which could be converted into grants for investment in industry or in hotel construction projects.

The Valesco agrarian reform was unusual for Latin America in its comprehensive scope and the relative speed of its implementation, with the result that a higher percentage of land was transferred than anywhere in the continent outside Cuba. But the vast scale and bureaucratic complexity of the reform, and the lower priority it received as the regime moved to the right in the mid-1970s, meant that when the reform process was finally wound up in 1980 much less land had been transferred than originally planned. Many landowners, particularly on the coast, dodged the reform by splitting up their estates into medium-sized units and distributing their ownership among family members. In some cases this prompted strikes by hacienda workers and official intervention. In many cases hacendados sold off equipment and slaughtered animals before expropriation. Moreover, while the hacienda system had been politically dominant and had monopolised the most fertile land and water resources, the land it had physically occupied represented a minority of total land. On the coast a substantial number of small and medium farms were not subject to expropriation, while in the sierra the majority of the land was occupied by some five thousand campesino communities, although nearly all of this was of very poor quality, much of it high altitude rough pasture. By the time it was terminated the reform had affected only 39 per cent of total agricultural land, and only one farm animal in ten. Less than a quarter of the rural population benefitted from the reform, and four out of ten of these were members of campesino communities who in most cases did not receive land but only the indirect benefits of association with a SAIS. Consequently, the reform transferred no more than 1.5 per cent of national income, and nearly all of this went to the 100,000 permanent estate labourers who had previously been a relatively better off group in the countryside.

The delay in the execution of the reform in the southern sierra, and its marginalisation of the campesino communities, triggered mass invasions of hacienda lands by communities in the Andahuaylas region in 1974. As a result, the government was finally forced to allow the campesinos in this area to divide the land as they wanted rather than establish SAIS's.

Agricultural production continued to grow during the 1970s at the same slow rate that it had done for the previous decade, disproving the oligarchy's prophecy that reform would involve a catastrophic decline in agricultural efficiency. However, growth was restrained by the government's failure to combine land reform with a comprehensive agricultural policy involving higher producer prices and increased technical support and investment. Securing cheap food supplies for the urban population was an overriding priority for the military government since it feared urban discontent even more than rural poverty. As a result, imported foods were subsidised, depressing local prices for agricultural products. In addition, the internal problems of the collectivised enterprises contributed to the failure to achieve rapid production growth. As many agricultural engineers emigrated their functions were filled by often inefficient and obstructive state regulation, reducing the identification of the workers with the co-ops. Apart from the effects of decapitalisation by the former owners, the co-ops also had to finance social security payments and educational and health provision for the workers. These financial burdens for the enterprises, which represented improvements in living standards for their workers, meant that few SAIS's (many of which had been unprofitable as haciendas before the reform) were able to distribute profits to their associated communities.

Educational and Social Reform

Despite the expansion in the state educational budget under Belaunde, more than a quarter of Peruvian children never entered a primary school in 1971, while only a third started secondary education and even fewer completed it. Almost a third of the adult population was illiterate. Of these two million adult illiterates, seven out of ten were women, and the majority lived in rural areas. The Velasco government saw educational reform as a key to the modernisation of the country, and gave a small group of civilian radicals the job of reorganising the educational system. Led by Augusto Salazar Bondy, a philosopher belonging to the Social Progressive intellectual movement, they were influenced by Ivan Illich and Brazilian educationalist Paulo Freire. They aimed to replace the traditional Spanish academic bias of Peruvian education with a system that would integrate study with training for work and a curriculum that placed more emphasis on an understanding of underdevelopment. Peruvian children were previously taught more about European history than the pre-conquest history and culture of their own country. The preamble to the 1972 Educational Reform Law signalled the changed emphasis, stating that 'the educational process will awaken in the Peruvian people a critical awareness of their condition and stimulate them to participate in the historical process of removing old structures of dependence and domination.' The new curricula were strongly nationalist and Third World orientated. Co-education was introduced and text books supplied free of charge in poor areas. Velasco declared Peru to be a bilingual country and made Quechua a second official language. Under the reform, children were to be taught in Quechua, Aymara or jungle Indian languages if their parents wished.

The reformers planned to reorganise educational administration along participatory lines, with the involvement of factories, community organisations, students and parents, as well as local authorities. But the reform faced hostility on three fronts, and many of its more imaginative aspects were not fully implemented. The middle class felt threatened by the reform's attack on their academic aspirations for their children. The administrative reorganisation was sabotaged by education ministry officials, who were unsympathetic to the reform's radical aims. Equally, the government failed to involve teachers in the planning and implementation of a reform which for them meant more work for no extra pay. The Velasco government had a highly conflictive relationship with a powerful new teachers union (SUTEP), whose maoist leadership viewed the regime as a fascist dictatorship. The cooperation of teachers in the reform became impossible after a strike in 1973 resulted in the arrest of 400 teachers and a government refusal to recognise SUTEP. As the government moved to the right, the education budget was cut back, meaning, for example, that Quechua texts were not made widely available and bilingualism did not advance beyond government rhetoric (normally in Spanish).

In further social reform measures, Velasco extended the social security system, and introduced a subsidised basic medicines programme. Legislation was introduced regulating the working conditions of domestic servants. Domestic service remains the largest single source of employment of women in Lima. Many maids are young sierra migrants, and work long hours for low wages (averaging less than £20 a month in 1983) as well as often facing racist contempt and sexual harassment. However, since no enforcement machinery was established the law remained no more than a statement of good intentions.

Velasquismo and Mass Politics

Much of the regime's attention was devoted to attempts to expand its political base beyond the armed forces, but the relationship between the government and social and political organisations in the civilian world proved to be highly conflictive, provoking sharp divisions within the military itself. Although the regime's anti-oligarchic measures denied it support from the right and centre, Velasco was careful to distance himself from all political parties as such. However, the government was supported by the Christian Democrats, the Social Progressive intellectual movement, and also by the pro-Moscow Communist Party (PC-U), who saw it playing the role of a national bourgeoisie despite its open anti-communism. Individual members of these parties and APRA worked in the government at middle levels. The new left parties, on the other hand, were highly critical of the regime. For Vanguardia Revolucionaria the regime was 'bourgeois reformist with corporatist tendencies' — corporatism denoting an authoritarian neutralisation of class conflict and promotion of capitalist development by the state. Meanwhile, university halls rang with arcane debates as to whether the regime was 'fascist', as Sendero Luminoso argued, 'fascistoid' or 'proto-fascist', as other maoist groups maintained.

In an effort to by-pass the political parties, the regime attempted to mobilise support among workers, campesinos and shanty town dwellers, but its efforts to do so were authoritarian and unsuccessful. The government was trapped between the need for mass support to sustain its reformist programme and its desire to control mass mobilisation and prevent radicalisation of the reforms. This dilemma meant that the government refused to trust genuinely democratic mass organisations and became increasingly anti-communist. 'Every time they set up an organisation it was captured by the left and then closed down', was how a Velasco aide put it.

The first attempt to establish a political base outside the armed forces was the setting up of Committees for the Defence of the Revolution in 1970. However, their Cuban-derived name and their domination by the left meant that they were quickly disbanded. At the same time, attempts by progressive officers to politicise the army rank and file with courses on marxism and social theory were squashed. A more systematic attempt to promote and control popular mobilisation began with the formation of the National System for the Support of Social Mobilisation (SINAMOS) as a government agency in 1971. It was charged with political organisation and technical support for campesinos and shanty town residents. General Leonidas Rodriguez, a leading progressive officer who as a colonel had planned the 1968 coup, was appointed director of SINAMOS. While its staff initially included a number of civilian radicals, it soon clashed with class-based campesino organisations and the parties of the radical left who were organising in the same fields. SINAMOS's task was to control and conciliate in the name of 'participation' and 'self-management' at a time when reforms were increasing class conflict.

SINAMOS set up a new agricultural mass organisation, the Confederacion Nacional Agraria (CNA), based on the cooperatives and the SAIS. The CNA was an attempt to rival the CCP, which was critical of the agrarian reform's neglect of the campesino communities. The CNA gained a representative base in the new agricultural enterprises, but as dissatisfaction with the regime's agricultural policy spread it broke free from SINAMOS's control and was eventually deprived of official support.

In the shanty towns SINAMOS adopted a more sophisticated version of the paternalistic approach followed by every government since Odria, distributing of food and building materials in return for political loyalty. SINAMOS set up a political network reaching down to street level. The granting of land titles and financial and technical support for the installation of water, sewerage and electricity were made conditional on the acceptance of SINAMOS's organisational control, causing widespread resentment. The government initially adopted a tough line on new land invasions, but a change of policy was forced by a massive land seizure by tens of thousands of homeless people at Pamplona Alta in Lima's 'southern cone' in 1971, when one squatter was killed and fourteen wounded by the police. The government relocated the squatters to a stretch of desert on Lima's southern edge, where they founded Villa El Salvador. Officially designated a 'self-managing city', the government promised to finance cooperative workshops on the site to provide employment. The pledge was not fulfilled, and in 1984 many of Villa El Salvador's population of 250,000 were still having to spend four hours a day on crowded buses to find work in Lima.

Industrialisation and the relatively tolerant political climate of the late 1950s and early 1960s had prompted a resurgence of the trade union movement. The number of officially recognised workplace unions grew fivefold between 1955 and 1968 to reach 2,317. Meanwhile, Aprista domination of the unions had been undermined with the faltering of real wage growth as the export boom drew to a close. The APRA-dominated CTP espoused 'free trade unionism', working in close cooperation with the American Institute for Free Labour Development (later revealed to be a CIA front), and hundreds of CTP leaders received training in the US. In these circumstances, PC-U influence in the unions increased and on the eve of the Velasco coup several important union federations left the CTP to form a new national confederation. This took the name of the Confederacion General de Trabajadores Peruanos (CGTP), imitating the union federation formed by Mariategui forty years earlier. Like its predecessor, the dominant force in the new CGTP was the PC-U. By 1972 the CGTP claimed a membership of 400,000 workers, and the majority of the major unions were affiliated. A small Christian Democrat-inspired union confederation, the Confederacion Nacional de Trabajadores (CNT), was also established, leaving the CTP with the sugar workers, dockers, drivers, private clerks, and part of the textile workers as its only significant affiliates.

The Velasco government's search for political allies meant that it initially adopted a conciliatory approach to the unions. The labour stability law and the labour community strengthened the unions' position, and the number of officially recognised unions increased to 4,330 by 1975. However, in what proved to be the first initiative of a corporatist tendency within the regime, Industry Minister Admiral Alberto Jimenez de Lucio and Fisheries Minister General Javier Tantalean launched a government-sponsored trade union con-federation, the Central de Trabajadores de la Revolucion Peruana (CTRP) in 1972. The launching of the CTRP from the industry ministry, bypassing SINAMOS, was an attempt to challenge the dominant influence of the PC-U and new left parties over the trade union movement. The CTRP received government money and recognition as well as the support of the police and a shady organisation known as the Movimiento Laboral Revolucionaria (MLR). The personal vehicle of Tantalean, the MLR was principally composed of gangster elements recruited from the underworld of Callao. Employing bribery and violence, the MLR gained control of the fishermen's union, but most of the CTRP's other affiliates only existed on paper. When labour unrest grew in the mid-1970s the MLR devoted itself to organising strike-breaking, while the PCP's continuing support for the government meant that the CGTP leadership attempted to restrain militancy. In these circumstances, the influence of the new left parties in the unions grew, and important unions (such as the miners) began to leave the CGTP. Together with the teachers' SUTEP, which had remained outside the CGTP, these unions formed an independent block and adopted an increasingly combative stance towards the regime.

5 The System in Crisis

By the mid-1970's the 'Peruvian revolution' had reached a cross-roads: it could either opt for a decisive radicalisation of the reforms backed by popular mobilisation, or it could return to the path of capitalist orthodoxy and seek business and middle class support. The immediate pressures on the regime to define itself arose from its fruitless search for a solid base of popular support as well as from the growing economic crisis. These problems punctured the public facade of military unity as rival factions fought over the direction of the revolution. These internal divisions coincided with and partly reflected a reorganisation of the civilian right as industrialists, medium-sized commercial farmers and professional associations attempted to restrict the reforms to limited anti-oligarchic measures. These groups felt threatened by what they saw as a growing radicalisation involving an abandonment of free enterprise in favour of a state-controlled economy. This fear, crystallised under the banner of anti-communism, was taken up by the daily press and a group of conservative military officers headed by Navy Minister Admiral Luis Vargas Caballero. Together with many of his naval colleagues, Vargas Caballero supported a rapid return to civilian rule, which both Accion Popular and APRA were demanding. This first major conflict within the armed forces came to a head when Velasco fell seriously ill in 1973 and was hospitalised for an operation to amputate a leg. Vargas Caballero and his supporters pushed for Velasco's replacement, and became outspoken in their public allegations of communist penetration of the government. However, Velasco was supported by both the progressive officers and a group, headed by Tantalean, whose primary loyalty was to the president himself. This support enabled Velasco to force Vargas Caballero and many of his naval colleagues in the government into retirement in 1974, and then to expropriate the daily press. The government had previously

Jose Carlos Mariategui.

Victor Raul Haya de la Torre.

General Juan Velasco Alvarado.

General Francisco Morales
Bermudez.

Hugo Blanco.

Fernando Belaunde Terry.

Alfonso Barrantes.

Agriculture in the Sierra.

Campesino mobilisation in the Sierra.

The Informal Economy at work, Cuzco. Camila Jessel

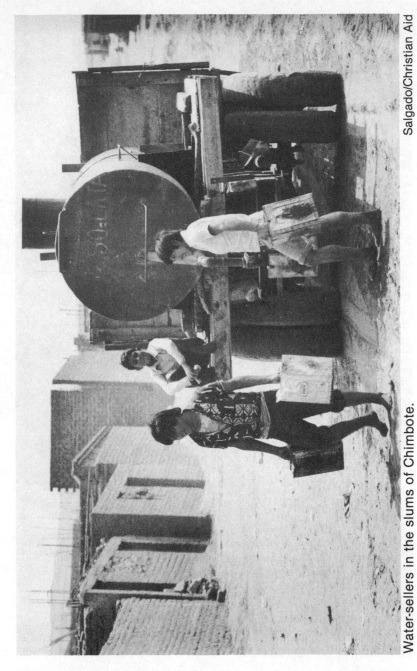

Water-sellers in the slums of Chimbote.

Salgado/Christian Aid

General Strike 19 July 1977.

61

Alleged members of Sendero Luminoso in El Fronton Prison.

nationalised two tabloid dailies, *Correo* (in the take-over of the Prado interests) and *Expreso* (owned by Belaunde's Prime Minister Manuel Ulloa, whose links with the Rockefellers made it a symbolic target for expropriation) and the two commercial television stations (owned by close collaborators of Belaunde). The rest of the daily press had, however, remained in the hands of the oligarchy. The legislation expropriating the press envisaged that after a transitional period in which the papers were run by government-nominated editors, they would be turned over to popular organisations representative of sectional interest groups, such as teachers and trade unions. In a calculated snub to oligarchic tradition, the CNA campesino organisation was to take control of *El Comercio*, the Lima equivalent of *The Times*. However, the regime's subsequent rightward drift meant that these plans were shelved. Progressive journalists and editors appointed at the time of expropriation were subsequently fired, censorship was imposed, and the media became a vehicle for government propaganda.

By 1974 the Peruvian economy was suffering from faltering growth rate, rising inflation, growing food shortages, and a large balance of payments deficit. The government had failed to mobilise internal sources of finance for its ambitious programme of industrial, irrigation and mining projects, and the activities of the newly-formed state corporations. Private investment declined because of business hostility to the reforms, while tax increases and measures to halt capital flight were not implemented for fear of middle class opposition. The government funded food subsidies by printing money and used foreign loans to pay for its investment projects. In view of the US-inspired embargo on subsidised loans from multilateral agencies to Peru, the government turned to the international banks, which were desperate to unload their mountains of 'petrodollars'. The public sector foreign debt doubled between 1972 and 1975 as the government's investment projects reached the spending stage, and debt service payments ate up an increasing share of export earnings. As a result, Velasco's efforts to increase Peru's economic autonomy only integrated the country even more closely with the world economy since exports had to be increased to repay foreign loans and to buy the imported machinery needed to develop heavy industries. Yet Peru's export earnings were declining, hit by falling world prices in the wake of the 1973 oil crisis as well as by delays in the exploitation of the crucial Cuajone copper mine and of jungle oil resources.

This balance of payments crisis broke at a time when Peru was diplomatically isolated in Latin America since Valasco had entered into diplomatic relations with Cuba and the Eastern Bloc countries, and Peruvian diplomats assumed a leading role in the non-aligned movement. Although the US remained Peru's major trading partner, the government sought closer trade relations with the Soviet bloc, and the Soviet Union and Eastern European countries became involved in several major development projects. After the overthrow of the Allende government in Chile, the US sought to present the Velasco regime as the beach-head of Soviet communism in South America, and fomented border tension with Chile. This stimulated a major programme of arms purchases from the Soviet Union, including an order for more than 200 Soviet tanks, which both increased Peru's indebtedness and fuelled the hostility of the US and the right-wing military dictatorships of South America. Moderate military officers began to see this continental hostility to the 'Peruvian revolution' as threatening to national security, increasing their concern to limit the reformist process.

The Fall of Velasco

Following his illness, and as the conflicts within the military sharpened, Velasco became increasingly autocratic. The officers who had supported him against the naval conservativies themselves divided into conflicting factions. Tantalean's group, known as 'La Mision', took up the anti-communist banners of the defeated navy faction. La Mision controlled the key political ministries and government agencies, and stepped up its campaign against left-dominated popular organisations in the name of an increasingly authoritarian personality cult around Velasco. Tantalean manoeuvred to convert the MLR into the permanent political expression of the 'Peruvian revolution', into which other mass organisations would be absorbed. He was opposed by the progressive officers led by Leonidas Rodriguez and Energy Minister General Jorge Fernandez Maldonado. They favoured the formation of a Velasquista political party based on the CNA, the labour communities and SINAMOS-sponsored organisations, but also including independent groups who supported the reformist process. The progressive officers supported the extension of the reforms while La Mision saw the military's revolution as complete. Velasco gave veiled backing to La Mision and his speeches became increasingly anti-communist in tone. In these circumstances, Lima was shaken by riots on 5 February 1975 in which more than 200 people were killed. The riots took place during a police strike, and were led by Aprista agitators and criminal elements; the involvement of the CIA has also been alleged. As the president's support for La Mision became increasingly evident, and popular discontent over the deteriorating economic situation mounted, the progressive officers moved into an alliance with a group of moderate military leaders headed by Prime Minister and Army Commander General Francisco Morales Bermudez. In August 1975, Morales Bermudez staged a bloodless coup against Velasco, whose removal produced no popular reaction.

Military Rule Mark II

Like Valasco, Morales Bermudez enjoyed a high professional reputation within the armed forces. Trained as an economist, he had run the finance ministry in a technically competent manner from 1969 to 1974 but most of the initiatives for economic reforms had come from other government departments. By 1975 Morales Bermudez had come to head an 'institutionalist' group which was aligned neither with La Mision nor the progressives but who were worried by Velasco's increasing caudillismo and the international pressures that the 'Peruvian revolution' had generated. Installed in the palace, Morales Bermudez was quick to announce that the ideology of the regime had not changed 'one millimetre', and the appearance of continuity was maintained by the presence of the leading progressive officers in the new cabinet. However, in an important institutional change, Morales Bermudez reactivated the junta of armed service chiefs whose existence as the maximum authority of the regime had become largely formal under Velasco. The junta was composed of moderate officers, and its new status served to isolate the progressives in the cabinet. The restoration of an 'institutional' regime also meant that conservative naval chiefs returned to a full share in government. These moves demonstrated that the regime's sole political base lay in the armed forces. They also signalled a retreat from the reformist process and the abandonment of the search for support in the popular classes. In what Morales Bermudez called 'the second phase of the Peruvian revolution', in which 'deviations' would be corrected, the government moved to tackle the economic crisis with cuts in public spending and began to implement counter-reform measures. These included the conversion of the labour community into a simple profit-sharing scheme in the private sector; the dropping from official rhetoric of the primacy of the social property sector; the slowing of the agrarian reform programme; and the easing of restrictions on profit remittances by foreign companies.

The swing to the right was completed with the ejection of the progressive officers from both government and troop commands. Rodriguez was forced into retirement in October 1975. Prime minister Fernandez Maldonado and the remaining progressives in the cabinet followed in July 1976, pushed out by a barracks mutiny. Rodriguez formed the Partido Socialista Revolucionario (PSR), grouping together civilian radicals and military progressives who supported the continuation of the reformist process, but it was too late to stop the move to the right. In July 1976 a handful of middle-ranking PSR army officers attempted a coup, linked to a proposed popular uprising in Villa El Salvador. However, the action was poorly planned and carried out in isolation from the rest of the left, much of which was hostile to the Velasquistas. The episode merely served to make the PSR a central target in mounting repression directed by the hard-line Interior Minister General Luis Cisneros. The progressive officers' failure to override Velasco's opposition to the encouragement of popular mobilisation the previous year had cost them dear.

'Stabilisation' and Struggle

The most drastic policy reversal in the second phase was the adoption of a deflationary economic policy. By the end of 1975 the failure of Velasco's model was fully evident and Peru's economic difficulties were exacerbated by falling world prices for raw material exports. Imports soared to twice the level of exports. The public sector foreign debt had doubled in three years to reach US$3.5 billion and debt service absorbed 23 per cent of export earnings.

For the next three years, Morales Bermudez attempted to implement an orthodox 'stabilisation' policy to bring the economy back into equilibrium. This policy had three main elements. First, the reduction of real wages by cutting food subsidies and holding down wages with the aim of reducing the budget deficit and the need for foreign loans to finance it. Secondly, reducing public investment with the objective of decreasing demand for imported goods. Thirdly, the devaluation of the sol was intended to stimulate Peruvian exports by making them cheaper and to reduce imports by making them more expensive. Although Morales Bermudez agreed with the IMF's strategy for stabilisation which lay behind these measures, he faced the threat of rising social instability which the deflationary policy provoked. Therefore, in the belief that they would be more flexible than the IMF, Morales Bermudez approached a consortium of US commercial banks in March 1976 for a US$200 million loan to support the balance of payments. However, the banks (Citibank, Bank of America, Chase, Manufacturers Hannover, Morgan Garanty and Wells Fargo) drove a tough bargain. They wanted a 44 per cent devaluation, price increases and budget cuts, concessions to foreign capital (including the waiving of US$50 million of back taxes owed by

SPCC), and a cutback in the state sector, starting with the sale of the nationalised fishing fleet.

As a result, in June 1976 the government increased the petrol price by 100 per cent, food prices by 50 per cent and wages by only 10 to 15 per cent. Credit to the private sector was restricted and 'mini-devaluations' started. Nonetheless, the consortium refused to provide Peru with a new loan in 1977 unless it was underwritten by the IMF; the banks were concerned at criticism of their open interference in Peruvian economic policy-making. They also considered Morales Bermudez to be sufficiently secure to implement a tougher IMF-style deflationary programme.

In a complicated series of on-off agreements with the IMF during 1977 and 1978, Morales Bermudez and a succession of finance ministers implemented most of the measures the Fund required. These included the devaluation of the sol (which fell from 69.4 to the dollar at the end of 1976 to 196.2 by the end of 1978); further fuel and food price increases; higher interest rates and cuts in the state investment programme. However, the government did little to dismantle the state enterprises, as both the IMF and local private industrialists wished. One reason for their survival was that they provided rich pickings for the high-ranking military officers who ran them.

The stabilisation policy had a drastic effect on production, wages and employment. Gross Domestic Product fell by 1.2 per cent in 1977 and 1.8 per cent in 1978. Since the population was growing by around 2.5 per cent a year, this implied a per capita fall of more than 8 per cent for the two years. Manufacturing was badly affected by tightening credit and declining domestic demand as real wages fell. This led some industrialists to question the government's handling of the economy. The worst hit sectors were the most labour intensive. Official figures showed unemployment and under-employment rising from 45.8 per cent of the workforce in 1975 to 53.9 per cent in 1977. Real wages for those who still had stable jobs in the Lima area fell by around 50 per cent between 1974 and the end of 1978.

With the abandonment of price controls on all but a handful of basic products and sweeping reductions in subsidies, inflation soared to 70% by 1978. Food prices increased even more than the consumer price index as a whole. The result was that hunger and malnutrition increased sharply. A study of low income families showed that average daily calorie intake fell by 22 per cent between 1972 and 1979 to only 62 per cent of the internationally recommended minimum level. Meat disappeared from the tables of shanty town families, while milk became a rarely consumed luxury. They were replaced by Nicovita, a synthetically produced chicken feed which was eaten by growing numbers of the poor, despite reportedly causing fibrous growths on the lungs.

Despite the considerable human cost of 'stabilisation' the public sector deficit remained high. Government spending on health and education was cut but arms purchases from abroad were increased. Defence spending had begun to increase under Velasco, particularly after the overthrow of the Allende government in Chile. Since Morales Bermudez become almost universally unpopular when the stabilisation policy took effect, he felt it necessary to strengthen his political base within the military by satisfying their demands for modern equipment. As a result, by 1977 official defence spending was 7.3 per cent of GDP and accounted for a large portion of both the public sector and balance of payments deficits.

The working class responded to the unprecedented reduction in living standards and the dismantling of much of the participatory apparatus introduced by Velasco with a series of strikes. After the June 1976 economic package a transport strike and street demonstrations were met by a country-wide state of emergency. Its provisions prohibited all strikes, restricted collective bargaining, suspended constitutional guarantees of freedom of assembly, permitted arrests and house searches without a judicial order, and imposed a 10.00 pm to 5.00 am curfew in Lima and Callao. Nevertheless, strikes continued. The fishermen's union, which had purged itself of the fascist elements from the MLR, struck for 54 days in protest at the reprivatisation of the fishing fleet. Generous compensation had been paid to the bankrupt fishmeal companies when the fleet was nationalised after the collapse of the fishmeal boom; the denationalisation of the fleet coincided with a revival of fishing activity. The fishermen received little support from the rest of the trade union movement — the PC-U leadership of the CGTP still supported the government — and were defeated, with 10,000 workers being sacked. According to union sources, there were 32,000 sackings in 1976 alone in Greater Lima under the provisions of the state of emergency.

As the unions attempted to defend economic and political gains they had made over the previous years, a broad but loose 'popular' movement developed. This brought together students, a dozen or more small left-wing parties, sections of the Catholic Church, shanty town communities, peasant organisations and small traders. These groups frequently gave active support to striking trade unionists, but they also took the lead in many spontaneous regionally-based protests, often taking the form of local general strikes (in which small business as well as unions took part) accompanied by sometimes violent street demonstrations. These protests often gave rise to ad hoc regional defence committees.

Popular protest was met with repression as the government acquired the characteristics of a traditional military dictatorship. This response, and the fact that the state was by far the largest single employer, gave labour conflicts a highly political character. For the unions, the restoration of democratic freedoms became as important a demand as traditional issues involving wages and dismissals.

Repression gave rise to a greater degree of coordination amongst the unions, yet this was not translated into a greater political unity since the left-wing parties remained badly divided. Often they trailed in the wake of spontaneous popular anger against the dictatorship rather than leading it. Political sectarianism was also reflected in the fragmentation of the trade union movement. Unions were grouped nationally according to the political affiliations of their leaderships. The CGTP was kept under firm control by the PC-U, which maintained a policy of 'critical support' for the regime that resulted in important unions, such as the miners and the majority of the metalworkers, leaving the CGTP. Other major unions, such as SUTEP (teachers), the power workers and the CCP peasant federation remained independent. These 'clasista' (class conscious) unions, mainly controlled by members of radical left parties, grouped themselves into the Coordinating Committee for Trade Union Unity (CCUS). Meanwhile, the bulk of the CTRP, the CNA peasant federation and the Christian Democrat CNT moved into opposition to the government. The CTRP split, the majority oppositional wing calling itself the CTRP-Lima.

Under the 1976 emergency, which was to last for over a year, all weekly magazines were frequently closed down and leading left-wingers were swiftly deported. Augusto Zimmerman, Velasco's press secretary, was forced into hiding in the Panamanian Embassy and a book he had written on the Velasco years was suppressed on publication. Velasquista middle-ranking military officers were exiled, as the strains within the armed forces intersified. The mere declaration of a strike led immediately to arrests of union leaders and mass sackings. Left-wing parties were forced into semi-clandestinity. However, the repression was selective, aimed particularly at rank and file leaders. Detentions were normally for short periods, but often repeated several times. Some union leaders disappeared: sometimes they re-appeared alive, but on other occasions their corpses were found dumped by roadsides. However, this campaign did not match the full-scale internal war then taking place in Argentina and previously in Chile, Uruguay and Brazil. Discredited after almost a decade in power, the military regime lacked the whole-hearted support of the civilian right which a 'Pinochetazo' would have required. Equally, the young and divided Peruvian left did not pose as serious a threat to the capitalist order as their counterparts in the southern cone.

Student protests were dealt with equally toughly. Several students at the National Engineering University in Lima were killed after 300 students occupied the university campus in August 1976. In February 1977, armed police shut down the Teachers' Training University at La Cantuta, near Lima, a stronghold of the Patria Roja party. More than 600 students were arrested, one of whom died under torture. La Cantuta remained closed for almost four years.

In June 1977, a further 'package' of price rises brought resistance to the regime's economic policy to a new peak. A spontaneous wave of protest swept the country. Regional general strikes lasting several days took place in important provincial centres. In Cusco, four demonstrators were killed by the police, while in a week of demonstrations in the Andean town of Juliaca thirteen people were killed and five wounded. A month later a national strike was called (see box).

The Constituent Assembly

The government reacted swiftly to the success of the strike. Seven hundred people were detained, including the general secretaries of the CGTP, CTRP and CNT, and the regime gave companies fifteen days in which they could sack workers they believed had organised the strike. An estimated 3,500 workers were fired, many of them being union militants.

However, the strike did force the regime to change tack. It froze prices, temporarily reversing some of the June economic measures. This caused the IMF to delay signing its stand-by agreement until November 1977, but while it allowed food subsidies and petrol prices to be maintained at their existing levels, the Fund required larger cuts in public investment to compensate.

Of more lasting importance, Morales Bermudez was obliged to announce a timetable for a return to civilian rule. This involved the calling of elections for a constituent assembly to draft a new constitution in mid-1978, to be followed by presidential and parliamentary elections in 1980. As part of this controlled return to civilian political activity, Morales Bermudez lifted the state of emergency in August 1977.

The constituent assembly elections gave the regime a chance to assess the strength of the civilian political parties without surrendering power to them. Morales and the military hierarchy favoured APRA to

The General Strike of 19 July 1977

The strike was called and coordinated by the Comando Unitario de Lucha (United Committee of Struggle), a broad front of trade union organisations. Initiated by five independent *clasista* unions, the CUL quickly received the support of the CNT and, following rank and file pressure on the leadership, the CGTP. The only significant trade union bodies that did not back the strike were the Aprista CTP leadership, SUTEP and the Centromin miners, controlled at that time by the maoist Patria Roja party. APRA supported the Morales Bermudez government, while Patria Roja's opposition to the strike derived from a sectarian refusal to cooperate with 'revisionist' currents within the trade union movement.

The demands of the strike were circulated clandestinely in a leaflet:

'. . . We declare our firm rejection of the economic measures implemented by the government, whose object is to unload the economic crisis onto the backs of the workers and the Peruvian people.

It is evident that these measures will result in a vertiginous rise in the cost of living and the freezing of salaries and wages. At the same time, the government is promoting a violent offensive against the rights and conquests of the working class to impose its anti-worker and anti-popular measures. Thus, it is continuing to restrict collective bargaining and it has suspended the right to strike, as a result of which the government and the bosses have unleashed a wave of provocations and sackings aimed at dictating a Law of Job Insecurity. At the same time, trade union organisations are being intervened, leaders are being persecuted and arrested with the intention of terrifying workers.

We declare our intention to defend energetically the rights and conquests we have gained. Therefore, we put forward the following Platform of Struggle.

(1) For a general increase in salaries and wages in accordance with the rise in the cost of living and against the Emergency Programme of (Finance Minister) Piazza.

(2) For the freezing of the prices of articles of basic necessity.

(3) For the respecting of annual bargaining claims, without ceilings or restrictions.

(4) For full respect for job security.

(5) For the re-instatement of all sacked workers. Freedom for those detained and return of those deported because of their trade union or social struggles.

(6) For unrestricted respect for democratic freedoms (lifting of the Emergency Law and curfew); respect for the right to strike; freedom of assembly, of the press, of organisation, expression, and demonstration. No to interference in the representative organisations of the workers.

(7) Solution of the critical situation facing the fishermen.

(8) For non-interference in peasant enterprises and the suppression of the agrarian debt.

(9) For non-interference in the universities.

. . . We call on all independent organisations and the rank and file of the CTP to join forces to carry forward this Platform of Struggle by means of THE NATIONAL STRIKE of our organisations on 19 July 1977.

Lima, July 1977.'

Despite a massive anti-strike propaganda campaign in the government-controlled media, the strike was successful. Large gatherings of shanty-town residents stopped buses leaving for the centre of Lima, the key to the success of a strike in the capital. 'The Central Highway is blocked by boulders in the factory zone of Vitarte. The Northern and Southern Highways are virtually impassable because of the rocks, bricks, treetrunks etc placed on the roadways. The three avenues which join Lima and Callao are impassable because of the presence of pickets. The new avenues which go into the shanty towns to the north and south of Lima, Avenida Tupac Amaru and Avenida Pachacutec, are effectively 'occupied' by the local population. In the streets in the city centre, workers and students' demonstrations are being held. The strike is successful. Almost without exception, large and medium-scale industry is paralysed. Only in small businesses is there any activity, but at a reduced level . . . In the district of Comas around midday, five people are shot dead by naval marines when they were trying to disperse the local population who were blocking traffic in the Avenida Tupac Amaru. Another person died in a clash with the police in Vitarte.' (*Cronologia Politica* 1977)

succeed them, and the extended electoral timetable suited APRA and the right since it gave them time to revive dormant party organisations.

Although Accion Popular registered for the elections, Belaunde decided on his return from ten years of exile in the United States that the party should boycott the poll. Uncertain of his electoral strength, this was a calculated gamble on Belaunde's part, but it did enable him to appear in the 1980 presidential elections as a consistent and principled opponent of the military government. In AP's absence, the

PPC received the full backing of private business and the upper middle class, and launched an expensive US-style campaign. APRA, despite its close links with Morales Bermudez, felt forced to distance itself from the government, presenting itself as the 'democratic left'.

For much of the left the election call came as a surprise. Parties such as Vanguardia Revolucionaria considered the clash between the dictatorship and the 'popular movement' as amounting to a revolutionary situation. The PC-U and the Christian Democrats saw a new constitution as threatening the structural reforms carried out under Velasco. Nevertheless, the election campaign enabled the left to break out of the isolation into which it had been forced by the state of emergency. In January 1978, two left-wing electoral fronts were formed. The first, the Workers, Peasants, Students and Popular Front (FOCEP), brought together the two main trotskyist parties (the PST, led by Hugo Blanco, and POMR), the small pro-Albanian maoist party Bandera Roja, and an independent group headed by labour lawyer Genaro Ledesma. The second front, Democratic and Popular Unity (UDP), included the most important factions of Vanguardia Revolucionaria, both wings of the PCR, three of the half dozen groups into which the MIR had split, and nine minor sects. Mariategui and Mao were the main ideological influences on most of the groups making up the UDP. However, Patria Roja, then the largest maoist party in Peru, though internally divided, decided to boycott the 'electoral farce'.

In formal terms, the government conducted the election campaign democratically. The election rules allowed 18 year-olds to vote for the first time, but excluded 2 million adult illiterates. The left was allowed to register and was given television time and newspaper space along with the right-wing parties. But at the same time the government campaigned vigorously against left-wing 'subversion' and gave scarcely veiled support to APRA. After Hugo Blanco called for the dissolution of the armed forces, FOCEP and the UDP were denied further access to the media.

The election campaign took place against a background of continuing confrontations between government and the unions. The sackings in the wake of the general strike had forced the unions on to the defensive during the second half of 1977, and the re-instatement of those who had been sacked became the main demand of the unions, supported by the Church and the left-wing parties. However, the union leadership was divided on how to achieve it. The CGTP backed out of a further general strike planned for January 1978, being partly influenced by a government call for national unity following a border skirmish with Ecuador. This was neither the first nor the last time that frontier incidents were manipulated to defuse internal tension. A general strike was finally called in February, but it had little impact.

Having refused to obey the government's order that they re-hire sacked union militants, the private industrialists forced the enactment of a drastic modification to the Velasco job security law in March 1978. This new law gave employers unlimited power to sack workers until they had completed three years' service, making it much more difficult for the unions to organise. Nevertheless, strikes continued to break out. At the end of 1977, a fifty-day strike at Chimbote steel works had attracted massive demonstrations of support by the local population, and won a wage increase. In May 1978, SUTEP began a strike that was to last for 81 days, the longest national strike in Peruvian labour history (see box).

The SUTEP Strikes

The SUTEP teachers' union, the largest single trade union in Peru with around 100,000 members, was one of the most militant in its opposition to the military government. SUTEP had been dominated since its foundation in 1972 by the Patria Roja maoist party, whose emphasis on the role of middle class and intellectual groups in the revolutionary transformation of Peru echoed the concern of the teachers for greater recognition of their social and professional status. Almost half of all government employees were teachers, and their salaries formed a major component of government expenditure. As public spending was cut by Morales Bermudez, the purchasing power of teachers' salaries fell by almost half between 1976 and 1979, when a teacher with less than 15 years service earned around £50 a month. In addition, the cuts meant that school buildings and teaching resources, which had always been inadequate, deteriorated further.

In May 1978, SUTEP began a national strike which was to last for 81 days. The union wanted wage increases, the reinstatement of teachers sacked during previous strikes, and official recognition of the union. Strikes by public employees were illegal under the 1933 constitution, and since the regime feared the political radicalism of the union leadership police repression of the strike was heavy. The strike ended with the government conceding the teachers' demands. However, as in many other cases, the regime failed to fulfil its promises, and in June 1979 the teachers struck again. This second strike was even longer and more conflictive than the first. SUTEP mobilised widespread and militant popular support, particularly in

▶

provincial towns and cities where teachers have often played an important political role in expressing local grievances. Six members of the National Committee of Parents Associations went on hunger strike, as did left-wing members of the constituent assembly, while several other unions staged 24-hour solidarity strikes.

The government responded by declaring a state of emergency, and Education Minister General José Guabloche refused to negotiate with SUTEP, calling its leaders 'agitators and criminals'. In the course of the strike 30 people, including teachers, parents and school students, were killed, and more than 50 people hospitalised as a result of attacks by riot police during daily marches and mass meetings throughout the country. The president of the Teachers Cooperative Fund, Abel Callirgos, fell to his death from a fifth floor window while being interrogated by the police. More than 800 teachers were arrested and 3,000 sacked during the strike.

The teachers were finally driven back to work at the end of September with a wage increase of only around £7 a month and with SUTEP still unrecognised. Seven thousand teachers were not given their jobs back and joined the thousands of sacked trade unionists who were eking out a living as street vendors or, in more fortunate cases, taxi drivers. However, the strike had been important in strengthening the links between the unions and broader local protest movements.

In the final days of the election campaign a new 'package' of economic measures brought the clash between the dictatorship and the 'popular movement' to a new pitch of crisis. In the preceding months the government had avoided further deflationary measures in an effort to undermine the electoral appeal of the left. This had led the IMF to cancel its second stand-by agreement in February 1978. Morales had no alternative economic policy, and with Peru on the brink of defaulting on its foreign debt, he resumed negotiations with the Fund. The measures he introduced in May 1978 were intended to clear the way for a new agreement, cutting back state subsidies so that food, fuel and public transport prices were doubled.

Disorders swept the country in a violent and spontaneous wave of popular outrage. The major union organisations called a general strike for May 22 and 23. This time the strike was supported by SUTEP (the teachers were still on strike) and the miners. Realising that its membership was going to support the strike, the Aprista CTP leadership gave its backing at the last moment.

The government postponed the constituent assembly elections from 4 June to 18 June, declared a states of emergency and closed the weekly magazines. Blaming the strike on 'extreme left agitators' the ministry of interior ordered house raids and detentions of union leaders and left-wing politicians. However, the strike was virtually unanimous, support for it exceeding that of July 1977. In clashes in the Lima shanty towns the police killed an unknown number of local residents, while four people were killed in the Andean mining town of Huancavelica. At least 500 people were arrested during and immediately after the strike. On 25 May, by arrangement with the Argentine military junta, 13 left-wing leaders were deported to a military prison camp in northern Argentina. The deportees included PSR leaders Generals Leonidas Rodriguez, Arturo Valdez, and Admirals Larco and Faura; Hugo Blanco, Genaro Ledesma, and Ricardo Napuri from FOCEP; and Javier Diez Canseco, Ricardo Diaz Chavez and Ricardo Letts of the UDP. All of them were candidates in the elections. After holding them for several days, the Argentines permitted the deportees to seek asylum in third countries.

The constituent assembly elections took place in this atmosphere of repression. Leonidas Rodriguez, who had slipped back into the country, was arrested in the act of voting, as were two PU-C candidates and one from FOCEP. However, despite all the government's manoeuvres, and their own divisions, the left parties obtained 30 per cent of the vote, by far the highest left-wing vote in Peruvian electoral history. FOCEP headed the left vote with 12.3 per cent — a tribute to Blanco's charisma and record as a combative leader rather than an endorsement of his trotskyist politics. APRA, with 35.3 per cent of the vote, was the largest single party in the assembly, while the PCP vote swelled to 23.7 per cent in the absence of Accion Popular.

Political Consolidation and Economic Recovery

The election of the constituent assembly with its centre-right majority defused much of the political turmoil of the previous three years. While strikes and mobilisations continued, May 1978 proved to be the peak of the 'popular movement'. This was in part because the assembly marked an important step on the military's road back to barracks — the one aim which united the fragile coalition of interest groups which made up the 'popular movement'. The assembly also provided an institutional forum for the revival of conventional party politics, deflecting activity from the more explosive venue of the streets. Three years of repression and sackings had also worn down the unions and the left. The mass protests against the dictatorship had been fuelled by a potent but spontaneous mixture of anger and desperation. Unaccompanied by a unified and deeply-rooted political organisation, these were insufficient to confront more complicated political circumstances.

The regime was also helped by a boom in the prices of Peru's major exports which assisted Finance Minister Javier Silva Ruete and Manuel Moreyra, President of the Central Bank, appointed in May 1978. Both were technocrats with Aprista leanings, and they applied the stabilisation programme with greater technical and political skill than their predecessors. After three years in which the government had merely lurched from one foreign exchange crisis to another, Silva Ruete and Moreyra adopted a medium-term strategy for traditional export-led growth. Mini devaluations were stepped up, and larger quantities of subsidised credit made available to exporters, both of traditional raw materials and of 'non-traditional', or manufactured goods. Helped by these measures, non-traditional exports more than doubled in 1979, accounting for more than fifth of total exports. This gave some backing to the claims of ADEX, the exporting industrialists' association, that Peru's future lay with the 'Taiwan model' of manufacturing exports based on cheap labour and 'enterprise zones' for foreign capital. However, apart from textiles, canned fish, and chemicals, most non-traditional exports were partly processed minerals rather than finished consumer articles.

The boom in world prices for Peru's traditional raw material exports was even more important than the growth of manufactured exports in the turn-around in the balance of payments. Key investment projects, such as the trans-Andean oil pipeline and the Cuajone copper mine, finally came on stream so that Peru was able to expand production just when prices were rising. Oil and copper exports more than doubled in 1979, and the trade balance moved from a US$120 million deficit in the first half of 1978 to a massive US$1.6 billion surplus in 1979.

However, Silva Ruete and Moreyra used the foreign exchange brought in by the export boom to repay part of Peru's foreign debt ahead of schedule rather than to re-activate the local economy. They had signed a new IMF agreement in September 1978, involving further cuts in food subsidies and a credit squeeze for non-exporting companies.

The labour movement staged a series of defensive strikes against yet further reductions in the standard of living. A national miners' strike in August and September 1978 was defeated after 32 days, and so the miners were denied any significant share in the windfall profits the price boom gave the mining companies. A three day general strike called by the CGTP in January 1979 for the reinstatement of those made redundant also failed. This time APRA supported the government, and there was inadequate coordination between the

CGTP and the independent unions. Once again, the government imposed a state of emergency before the strike, rounding up union leaders and closing down the left-wing magazines. The strike was abandoned after two days.

However, in June 1979, the SUTEP teachers began a second national strike which escalated into a major confrontation with the regime (see box). The government attempted to isolate the teachers by decreeing a general wage increase for all employed workers, but combined this with a further round of price increases on basic products, that pushed inflation in the first six months of 1979 to 40 per cent. This package prompted the CGTP, the CNT and the independent unions to call the fifth general strike in two years, but despite widespread support this failed to force the regime to accept SUTEP's demands.

The left had also been kept at bay in the constituent assembly. In a characteristic marriage of convenience with the right, APRA gained control over the assembly by forming a working alliance with the PPC. Haya de la Torre, though mortally ill, was elected president of the assembly, the closest he came to the presidency of his country in a career which had dominated the political life of Peru for sixty years.

The APRA-PPC majority rejected left-wing calls to convert the assembly into a sovereign legislative body and limited it to the task of writing a new constitution. The major innovations in the document which Haya signed in July 1979, days before he died of cancer in a Texas clinic, were the abolition of the death penalty except in wartime, and the granting of the vote to all citizens over the age of 18. This enfranchised two million adult illiterates for the first time.

The Return of Belaunde

The upturn in the economy gave Morales Bermudez and Silva Ruete slightly more room for manouevre in the months preceeding the May 1980 elections which were held in a more peaceful social climate than had existed for the preceeding four years. Although the government-controlled media were required to give space to all political parties, as in 1978 they gave scarcely veiled backing to APRA until the final days of the campaign when it was clear that Belaunde would win.

Haya's death had thrown APRA into a complicated internal crisis. Most of the senior figures in the party, headed by Andres Townsend, favoured a continuation of Haya's conservative pro-US line of the 1950s and 1960s. They were challenged by a younger grouping, led by Armando Villanueva, that stood for a return to the rhetoric of the leader's radical youth. Villanueva was nominated as APRA's presidential candidate after a bitter conflict between the two factions culminated in a gun battle for physical control of the convention hall. His control over the party's organisational machine with its strong-arm 'defence squads' (known as 'bufalos') proved decisive, but gave him a poor public image. The internal feud and the party's close identification with the dictatorship destroyed APRA's chances in the elections.

The left suffered even more damaging splits after early hopes of greater unity. A short-lived electoral front involving the UDP, Patria Roja and other small groups associated with it, and two trotskyist parties (PRT and POMR) collapsed amidst bitter insults and recriminations. The front, known as the Alianza Revolucionaria Izquierdista (ARI, which means 'yes' in Quechua) had launched a charismatic presidential slate, headed by Hugo Blanco, with the former UDP president Alfonso Barrantes and SUTEP general secretary Horacio Zevallos as vice-presidential candidates. Much of the blame for ARI's self-destruction was justifiably levelled at the trotskyists. However, the agressive stance adopted by the maoist parties over the share-out of places in the congressional lists, and the vacillations of the UDP and Barrantes contributed to the debacle. The dissolution of ARI was a disaster for the left, which was now obliged to fight five separate, poorly financed and hastily organised electoral campaigns. Blanco, the best-known and most popular left-wing leader was marginalised and the trotskyists were excluded from future efforts towards left unity, shifting the left's point of balance towards the centre. A parallel attempt at coalition involving the PC-U, the Velasquista PSR and the rump of FOCEP around Ledesma also foundered. However, the PC-U and the PSR did run together as Unidad de Izquierda (UI) with Leonidas Rodriguez as their candidate.

The divisions in APRA and the left gave Accion Popular a clear field. Unlike the PPC, which was closely identified with the Lima elite, Belaunde was able to project a favourable image to a broad cross-section of society. As the victim of the 1968 coup, he presented himself as the anti-militarist candidate, the embodiment of civilian constitutional legitimacy in an election in which hatred of the military was the most powerful single ingredient. However, Belaunde focussed his criticism of the military regime on the Velasco period rather than the second phase, and he avoided any commitment to punish individual officers for their excesses. A master of sonorous rhetoric, Belaunde filled public squares up and down the country with pledges to create 'a million jobs in five years' and to expand food production by 'extending the agricultural frontier'. True to his party's symbol — a shovel — the architect and constructor Belaunde promised a major public works programme of roads and housing projects. He also enjoyed strong backing from the Carter presidency, which with its expressed commitment to human rights, saw an ideal ally in the conservative democrat.

The election result (see Appendix 4) gave Belaunde a clear margin of victory, with 45 per cent of the presidential poll. Villanueva failed to maintain APRA's customary third of the vote, and the party did poorly outside its traditional stronghold in the north. The PPC's Bedoya managed 10 per cent, polling weakly outside Lima. Many left-wing voters apparently opted for Belaunde in the presidential ballot as the lesser evil on the right, and the left-wing parties did rather better in the congressional than the presidential vote. But the division of their total congressional vote of 19 per cent (down 11 per cent on 1978) between five fronts meant that their parliamentary representation was small. The trotskyists and FOCEP, the PSR and PC-U were the main losers on the left compared with 1978. While the election was generally clean, only 64 per cent of the electorate cast valid votes, despite the fact that voting was compulsory. Seventeen per cent of the votes cast were classed as spoiled, many of them being disqualified for failing to meet strict requirements for filling in a complicated ballot slip. Although it aroused little interest at the time, the number of blank votes cast in the Andean departments of Ayacucho, Apurimac and Huancavelica was particularly high (15 per cent compared with a national average of 6 per cent). Sendero Luminoso had called for a boycott of the election, and in their first armed action, attacked a polling station in the remote Ayacuchan community of Chuschi.

6 Political Democracy and Economic Disaster

Opening Up the Economy

The country that Belaunde took over in July 1980 differed in fundamental ways from the one he had left so abruptly in 1968. The traditional ruling alliance between the agro-export oligarchy, the sierra gamonales, and foreign capital had been decisively broken by the Velasco reforms. In its place, a mixed economy and new centres of economic power had emerged. The state-owned sector of the economy accounted for 36 per cent of national production in 1980, double its 1968 share. Some 175 public corporations (compared with 18 in 1968) were responsible for the bulk of this production, and they included seven of the ten largest companies in Peru: Petroperu (oil); Electroperu and Electrolima (electricity); Centromin, Mineroperu and Minpeco (mining); Pescaperu (fishmeal); and Siderperu (steel). The state also controlled more than half of the financial system. However, the grip of foreign capital on the most profitable sectors of the economy remained strong. The three main oil and mining multinationals (Occidental Petroleum, Southern Peru Copper Corporation and Belco Petroleum) were the largest private companies in the country. But in the shadow of the Velasco reforms and the subsequent recession, Peruvian private capital had been obliged to reorganise itself. Powerful new business consortia had emerged, based in the financial system but also linked to agro-processing, export manufacturing and service sector companies. At the same time, an 'informal sector' of small and sometimes medium-sized businesses continued to grow outside the legal framework of taxes and bank credit, labour laws and trade unions. These operations employed an important section of the workforce in commerce, transport and small-scale manufacturing, sometimes acting as cut-price suppliers or distributors for large corporate businesses.

Belaunde and Accion Popular brought to this changed society little of their reformism of the 1950s and 1960s. The party had moved to the right, and its conservative bent was underlined when Belaunde again reached a coalition agreement with Bedoya's PPC to give the new government a parliamentary majority. The dominant figure in the government's first two and a half years was Prime Minister and Finance Minister Manuel Ulloa, an international businessman who had been Belaunde's finance minister in 1968. However, the government's approach to the economy was far from coherent. On the one hand, Belaunde remained a 'builder president', committed to high levels of state investment in roads, middle-class housing projects, and giant hydro-electric schemes. On the other hand, Ulloa appointed to the key economic posts young technocrats and bankers (many of them not party members) who favoured a sharp reduction in the state's role in the economy. Collectively known as 'The Dynamo', many of Ulloa's aides had spent years of voluntary exile during the military government working for US corporations or international financial institutions. Most of the members of the Dynamo had brought with them from the US an enthusiasm for neo-liberal economic policies, similar to those implemented by Pinochet's 'Chicago Boys' in Chile and, in a different context, by the Thatcher government in Britain. The Dynamo's free market strategy had three basic policies. First, they wanted to transfer resources to the private sector by selling off more than two thirds of the state companies. Secondly, they wanted to promote competition by eliminating subsidies and reducing state intervention in pricing, marketing, and the financial system. The Dynamo also sought to dismantle tariff barriers in order to expose local industry, which they considered to be largely inefficient, to foreign competition. Thirdly, they wanted to expand raw material exports (particularly minerals and oil) by offering more advantageous investment terms to both foreign and local private capital, backed up by state investment funded by foreign loans. These policies were to be accompanied by continuing mini-devaluations to maintain the international competitiveness of Peruvian exports.

These policies, which were supported by the World Bank and other international financial institutions, were directed towards encouraging the export of commodities that Peru could produce at comparatively low cost in international terms. The country could then use the foreign exchange from these exports to import goods which it could itself produce cheaply by world standards. The Dynamo argued that this would bring down inflation. However, in the real world, these policies meant the cementing of existing imbalances in economic power and the international division of labour.

Moreover, in the Peruvian context, the application of this doctrine of 'comparative advantage' involved a programme of structural change in the economy. In effect, it meant the abandonment of the state's experiments in nationally-based development and import-substitution industrialisation. Large parts of Peruvian industry, in both the private and state sectors, were certainly inefficient because they were producing for a small market, often with outdated technology and poor (and in state companies, sometimes corrupt) management. However, abandoning Peruvian industry to unrestricted competition from foreign-manufactured products (themselves often government-subsidised, or exported at 'dumping' prices) meant exposing the country completely to its traditional vulnerability to the international raw material markets. Since the world economy had entered a major recession in the mid-1970s, this was a recipe for disaster. Within two years of Belaunde taking office, raw material prices crashed to their lowest level since the 1930s, and Peru's balance of payments moved rapidly from boom to bust.

Ulloa and the Dynamo were working in the complex political environment of a representative democracy resting insecurely on a society marked by continuing extreme inequalities, which the free market drive itself tended to intensify. In these circumstances, the economic team's neo-liberal strategy ran into severe political problems and was only partially implemented. This was fully evident in the government's treatment of the state sector. While a new Industry Law abolished the state monopoly over basic industries, the government shrank from wholesale privatisation of state companies and banks. As technocrats and politicians close to the regime moved into well-paid jobs as directors and managers of the state corporations, they acquired a vested interest in defending their existence. However, government policies weakened many state companies by encouraging private sector rivals and starving state industries of investment funds.

In the face of the Dynamo's deflationary policies Belaunde's construction drive meant that state investment actually increased, the bulk of it going on public works and infrastructural projects linked to raw material export. In 1981 and 1982 half of public investment went to such projects, particularly large and often uneconomic hydro-electric schemes, for which international financing was still readily available. State-owned industry received only 2 per cent of public investment, compared with 20 per cent under Velasco. Some state industrial concerns, such as the profitable cement companies, were converted into mixed enterprises, with the private owners who had been expropriated by Velasco being awarded controlling shareholdings. In the steel industry the government supported the creation of a private-sector rival to the state-owned Siderperu. After unrestricted imports of poor quality 'dumped' steel weakened

Siderperu financially, the government moved to reduce its plant and workforce. Similarly, the bankrupt state-owned fishmeal company (Pescaperu) was drastically pruned, three-quarters of its plants being closed down and more than two-thirds of its 5,000 workers made redundant. The main beneficiaries were privately-owned fish canneries, using fish suitable for human consumption to make fishmeal. Other state companies, such as the Pepesca fish freezing and canning plant at Paita, a supermarket chain, and a machine tool and a tractor factory, both in Trujillo, were liquidated.

Given the opposition of the Dynamo to increasing taxes on private business, much of state spending was financed by foreign loans and by printing money. This weakened the balance of payments, and public sector deficits became as characteristic of the Belaunde government as they had been of the later years of the military regime in spite of the Dynamo's orthodoxies. When foreign loans dried up in 1983, these deficits began to suck money and credit from the private sector. Together with the removal of subsidies and the rising cost of credit they also drove inflation up.

Winners and Losers

Despite all its contradictions and inconsistencies, government policy clearly distributed both initial growth (1980-81) and subsequent deep recession (1982-84) unevenly between different sectors of private business. The chief beneficiaries were foreign and local finance capital. After a brief recovery in 1980, manufacturing industry producing for the local market began a dramatic decline, while agriculture remained stagnant.

Foreign capital was favoured by a new legal and administrative framework aimed at giving equal treatment to local and foreign investors throughout the economy. Foreign companies no longer had to 'Peruvianise' their shareholdings, and they were allowed to resume investments in banking, property development and commerce. The maximum amount of profit they could transfer home was doubled. This breached the Andean Pact's Decision 24 regulating foreign investment, and Peru pushed for the rule to be abolished. Foreign mining and oil companies benefitted from the phasing out of the 17.5 per cent tax on traditional exports, and were also exempted from many other taxes. Foreign mining companies were allowed to market directly rather than selling to Minpeco. The multinationals were also given greater access to unexploited mineral and oil deposits. As a result of all these measures, new foreign investment (mainly from the US) did increase briefly, but rapidly fell again as the world economy moved into recession. By 1984 more dollars were leaving the country in profit remittances than were entering in new investment. While half a dozen foreign oil companies, including Shell, signed exploration and development contracts, the results they reported were disappointing. Low mineral prices also meant that little interest was shown by foreign mining companies in developing new projects. As a result, the only important new mine developed under the Belaunde government — the Tintaya copper mine near Cusco — was run by the state.

However, foreign penetration of the economy was substantially increased as a result of the government's liberalisation of trade. All import bans and quotas were scrapped, and commercial vehicles for the politically-favoured transport owners were imported free of duty. The average tariff was cut to 32 per cent, the lowest level since 1964. Among the resulting flood of imports were greatly needed machinery and industrial raw materials, but luxury consumer goods (such as foreign cars and Scotch whisky for the Lima elite) also increased sharply. The abolition of selective import bans made smuggling of previously prohibited goods harder to detect, particularly because of corruption in the customs administration. Following pressure from industrialists and the PPC, and faced with the need to increase government revenue, Belaunde raised tariffs again in 1982 and duty-free imports were stopped. By then, however, the import boom had already badly damaged local industry. Thus, when the credit squeeze and the recession began in earnest many firms in the weakened industrial sector were pushed over the edge.

Manufacturing output fell by more than a fifth between 1981 and 1983, and by 1984 industry was operating at only 40 per cent of capacity. Textiles, vehicle assembly, engineering and leather goods were hit the hardest. The textile industry, the traditional core of Peruvian manufacturing, entered the worst crisis of its history. CUVISA, the fifth largest textile firm, went into liquidation, while Tejidos La Union, Peru's biggest industrial combine, registered its highest losses ever. Import liberalisation dealt a devastating blow to local vehicle assembly. The Peruvian-owned former Chrysler truck plant was forced to close, and Volvo assembled only ten vehicles at its Lima plant in the first half of 1983. Sales by the locally-based car assemblers Nissan, Toyota and Volkswagen, fell to less than half their 1981 level in 1983. Meanwhile, in industries such as shoes and garment-making, a large percentage of production was diverted to homeworkers in the 'informal' economy, increasing industrial unemployment and cutting government tax revenue. Moreover, manufacturing industry's difficulties were increased by its traditional reliance on credit (rather than share capital), and by inconsistencies in exchange rate policy. When the balance of payments was in surplus

Belaunde held down the exchange rate, over-ruling his liberal economic advisers and tempting many industrialists to contract dollar loans. As a result, when the rhythm of devaluation began to increase sharply in 1982, firms producing for the local market whose income was in soles were paying an effective interest rate of up to 150 per cent on their dollar loans.

While industry in general languished, finance capital (banks, finance corporations, and insurance companies) boomed. This was mainly because the rate of return on financial investments (principally currency speculation) was much higher than that from capital investment in the productive sector. This trend, the product of the depressed state of the internal market and the government's failure to tackle inflation, had begun under Morales Bermudez and accelerated under Belaunde as taxes on bank loans and commissions were scrapped and government regulation of interest rates was relaxed. Bank profits had increased by 39 per cent between 1975 and 1979. By 1981, the major private banks were averaging a return on capital of 25 per cent, while very few industrial companies were returning profits of more than 10 per cent of their capital. The privately-owned Banco de Credito, which was the largest Peruvian commercial bank with a third of the market, increased its net profit by a phenomenal 78 per cent to US$23.2 million in 1981. Two years later, with many of their industrial clients on the verge of bankruptcy, the banks were still returning large profits. However, the recession began to affect some of the less skillful banks, and their bad debts mounted. Two banks and their associated finance corporations were liquidated after uncontrolled lending, mainly in dollars, to companies associated with their directors. A third bank was nationalised to prevent its liquidation. The state paid out more than US$150 million to guarantee depositors' savings in these financial institutions while the in-criminated directors were allowed to slip abroad. Other banks, like the Credito, insulated themselves from the recession by cutting loans and moving liquid assets into dollars. With devaluations of the sol reaching 130 per cent in 1983, five points more than inflation, this was a profitable exercise.

Banks and finance corporations formed the lynchpins of several powerful private sector family-based economic conglomerates which had emerged during the military government and consolidated their dominant position under Belaunde. The largest and most powerful of these loose conglomerates was the Romero-Raffo group, based on the Banco de Credito, but with interests in insurance, property development, agro-industry, and export-oriented manufacturing (see box). The Romero-Raffo empire formed the spearhead of post-oligarchic capitalism in Peru. Politically more adept than the old

86

The Romero-Raffo Group

The Romero-Raffo group is the largest and most powerful private business empire in Peru. The group's rise since the mid-1970s illustrates the form in which Peruvian capitalism has adapted to the ending of the oligarchy's domination and the changes wrought by Velasco.

The group takes the form of a loose but carefully organised partnership between the Romero and Raffo families, held together by a complex web of interlocking directorships and cross-holdings of shares. Its substantial investments are concentrated in the most dynamic sectors of the contemporary economy: finance, agro-industry, and property development.

The group's powerbase is the Banco de Credito, which has an associated finance corporation and shares in two other local banks. Additionally, the Romero-Raffo empire includes majority holdings in two insurance companies (including El Pacifico, the largest in Peru), five property companies, two textile firms, two vegetable oil products factories, and an extensive palm oil plantation in the high jungle region. The group is one of the largest landowners in Lima, and recently built the capital's biggest US-style shopping centre at Camino Real in the affluent district of San Isidro.

The Romero and Raffo families both emigrated to Peru from Italy in the late nineteenth century. Part of the wave of immigrant entrepreneurs who played a prominent role in the nascent industrial development of the 1890s, they were among the founders of the Banco Italiano, which diplomatically changed its name to the Banco de Credito during the Second World War. The Romero's bought land in Piura, becoming important cotton hacendados. However, both families were essentially bourgeois in outlook with more flexible political attitudes than the traditional oligarchy. When the Romero cotton land was expropriated by the agrarian reform, the family moved into agro-processing, using their compensation to establish Textil Piura, a modern spinning plant.

In the 1970s, Dionisio Romero and Juan Francisco Raffo took charge of the group's business interests. Both were in their thirties, with college educations and business management experience in the United States. Unlike many traditional local manufacturers, they carried on investing during the military government. The reward for their political judgement came in 1979, when they organised a stockholder coup to take control of the Banco de Credito, in which they had only a 14 per cent share, from the Paris-based Sudameris banking group.

▶

Under Romero's and Raffo's management, the Credito became the largest and most profitable bank in Peru. It also became an international enterprise, opening branch offices in New York and the Bahamas, and an associated bank in the Cayman Islands. In 1984 it bought into the Valencia Bank of Orange County, California, with the aim of acquiring a majority shareholding. In 1983, around 20 per cent of the Credito's earnings came from its overseas operations. This share is likely to increase, as its prospects for growth in Peru are limited both by the recession and by the political sensitivity of its one third share of the local commercial bank market.

oligarchy, it exercised an important behind-the-scenes influence on policy-making under the Belaunde government without nailing its colours to a party mast. Like the oligarchy, having established a powerful base in Peru, it increasingly looked abroad for profits, either in the form of exports or the transfer of capital into investments overseas.

Crisis of the Century

After two years of moderate growth, the economy stood still in 1982 and collapsed in 1983, entering on what Manuel Ulloa called 'the worst economic crisis of the century'. Production fell by 12 per cent in 1983, while at the same time inflation leapt from its plateau of 70 per cent a year to 125 per cent. By mid-1984 there were few signs of recovery: production was stagnant while prices continued upwards. In part, the government could claim that the collapse stemmed from factors beyond its control. Natural disasters devastated much of the country in 1983, as a particularly strong El Nino current brought sustained flooding to the northern coastal desert, washing away much of the cotton crop and causing landslides throughout the northern and central Andes. At the same time, the south was hit by severe drought. These natural disasters were a major factor in the fall in agricultural output of eight per cent. The resulting scarcity of food increased prices.

Peru's economic collapse was also part of a wider Latin American drama that reached a temporary peak with the Mexican debt crisis in mid-1982. In the months after the Mexican shock, the flow of fresh foreign commercial bank loans, which had been propping up the balance of payments all over Latin America, abruptly dried up. This continental credit squeeze also followed a drop in raw material prices to rock-bottom levels as recession in the industrialised countries reduced demand. At the same time the OECD countries moved to protect their own vulnerable industries from Latin American and Asian competition. These factors meant that Latin American exports slumped, and an ever-higher proportion of the continent's export earnings was spent on debt service. Latin America became a net exporter of capital, and its economies plunged into recession. As huge public sector deficits in the United States (primarily the result of military spending) drove international interest rates up, the quota of popular sacrifice required for Latin America simply to keep up with its interest payments increased correspondingly.

The impact of these international factors was disproportionately severe in Peru. This was because the Dynamo's attempt to apply the theory of 'comparative advantage' in Peru had combined with Belaunde's loan-financed construction bonanza to weaken the balance of payments even before the debt crisis broke. The Dynamo eagerly promoted traditional raw material exports, but the fall in world prices for these products accounted for much of the 15 per cent fall in Peru's export earnings between 1980 and 1981. Meanwhile, tariff liberalisation, the over-valuation of the sol and project-tied equipment purchases triggered a doubling of imports between 1979 and 1981. These trends meant that in both 1981 and 1982 Peru's trade balance was US$550 billion in the red. On the other hand, although the government had criticised the rise in the foreign debt under the military regime, it continued to borrow abroad at the same rate as its predecessor. At a meeting with bankers and Western governments in Paris in 1981 Ulloa had sought up to US$4 billion for public investment projects. Large-scale arms imports also continued, culminating with the signing of a US$700 million contract for 26 Mirage interceptors in December 1982. Consequently, Peru's outstanding public sector long-term foreign debt grew from US$6.7 billion in 1980 to US$8.2 billion in 1983, while over the same period the total foreign debt grew from US$9.6 billion to US$12.4 billion. By 1982 service of the foreign debt was absorbing more than one dollar of every two earned in exports.

The Dynamo responded to the balance of payments problem by turning to the IMF. In June 1982, Ulloa and Central Bank President Richard Webb signed a three-year US$960 million agreement with the Fund. As well as shoring up the country's foreign accounts, the agreement was intended to support the economic team as its efforts to transform the economy along liberal lines faced rising opposition both within and outside the regime. The IMF policy recipe was by now highly familiar to Peruvians. Rather than impose selective import controls and crack down on capital flight, so that precious foreign exchange was used productively, the IMF agreement required the indiscriminate slashing of demand in the local market.

Monetarism and the Debt

Following the sudden resignation of Ulloa in December 1982, government economic policy swung further away from its earlier pragmatism towards an inflexible monetarism aimed at protecting the country's diminishing foreign exchange reserves at all costs. Ulloa's replacement as prime minister was Vice-President Fernando Schwalb, who had worked for the IMF from 1969 to 1976. The new finance minister was Carlos Rodriguez Pastor, an international banker who had lived in the US since 1968. He had risen to become executive vice-president in charge of the International Division of Wells Fargo Bank of San Franscisco, one of Peru's largest foreign creditors. Rodriguez Pastor installed former colleagues from Wells Fargo in his economic team, which quickly became known as 'La Diligencia', the stagecoach. Telling the press that he had 'not come to reactivate the economy', he cut public investment, speeded up the removal of those few subsidies that remained, accelerated the devaluation of the sol, raised interest rates and cut back the money supply. These measures contributed directly to the drop in production, the increase in the inflation rate, and a 20 per cent fall in real wages during 1983. Since much state spending was difficult to halt overnight, the private sector bore much of the weight of the squeeze.

Although imports fell by almost a third in 1983, a further fall in export earnings meant that Peru's debt repayment obligations outstripped the country's capacity to pay. In both 1983 and 1984, the government negotiated the postponement of repayments of debt principal with the commercial banks, OECD governments and the Eastern Bloc countries. But the cost of this debt rescheduling was high, comprising extra commissions and interest payments as well as committing the country to IMF-designed economic programmes that required further erosion of living standards. Despite its political affinity with its major creditors, and the docility of its diplomatic stance on the debt issue, the government did not gain better treatment than any of the other other, less tractable Latin American debtors in the rescheduling queue. Even after the rescheduling agreements Peru paid out more than four dollars of every ten earned from exports to cover debt service in 1983.

Despite Rodriguez Pastor's efforts, Peru repeatedly failed to meet the economic targets set by the IMF, which consequently rescinded the agreement in October 1983. This failure pointed to the self-defeating nature of the IMF's approach. The recession and an associated rise in tax evasion meant that government tax revenue fell by a third in 1983. Thus, despite a cut in government spending, the public sector deficit rose to an unprecendented 11.9 per cent of GDP rather than falling to 4.2 per cent as the IMF required.

With presidential elections scheduled for 1985, and as rising social discontent and Sendero Luminoso's guerrilla war undermined the regime's stability, government supporters became increasingly alarmed at the political price of austerity. Rodriguez Pastor negotiated a new draft agreement with the IMF, but he was rapidly losing ground within the government. The target of vitriolic criticism from many local manufacturers as well as the unions, the opposition and Accion Popular boss Javier Alva, his only supporters were the bankers, Prime Minister Schwalb, and Ulloa's dwindling band of followers in Accion Popular. His fate was sealed when a powerful group of ministers and officials, identified with neither Alva nor Ulloa, began to push for economic 'reactivation' and the mitigation of the social cost of austerity. Headed by Agriculture Minister Juan Carlos Hurtado Miller, this group was dubbed the 'Violeteros' since several of its leading members were relatives of Belaunde's wife, Violeta Correa Miller. Yielding to party, family and opposition pressure, Belaunde sacked Rodriguez Pastor in March 1984, and Schwalb quickly resigned. In a quixotic attempt to improve the government's image, Belaunde offered the premiership to his friend the novelist Mario Vargas Llosa, but a party revolt blocked the move. Instead, Sandro Mariategui, a senior AP politician and son of philosopher Jose Carlos Mariategui, became prime minister. Rodriguez Pastor was replaced by Jose Benavides, a 'Violetero' who had previously been minister of education and energy. Nothing in his career indicated that Benavides understood economics. The PPC took advantage of the cabinet reshuffle to leave the sinking government ship in preparation for the 1985 elections.

Having prepared the political ground for a rupture with the IMF and a reactivation of the economy, Belaunde and his new advisers shrank from the radical policies, such as a debt moratorium, that appeared to be the only alternative to orthodoxy. Benavides signed the draft IMF agreement negotiated by Rodriguez Pastor without achieving substantial modifications. The new 18-month emergency standby agreement involved an even tougher austerity programme than its discarded predecessor. Neither government officials nor the IMF staff appeared to believe that the agreement could be complied with, above all in an election year. It existed largely because of the US's mounting political concern that the radicalisation and instability produced by austerity and recession in Peru would push the country to default on its debts. Mariategui and Belaunde continued to talk of 'reactivation' but took no coherent steps to achieve it. Despite the reschedulings of 1983 and 1984, according to Central Bank President Richard Webb, the country faced debt interest payments of US$9 billion and a further US$9 billion in repayment of principal over the following five years. Unless a global political solution to Latin America's debt crisis was negotiated, Peru faced the stark choice of debt default or years of economic prostration.

Democracy and Injustice

The return to constitutional rule was accompanied by the restoration of formal democratic freedoms. Belaunde could also claim the distinction of being the only Peruvian president to organise democratic municipal elections, which were held in 1980 and again in 1983, as they were during his first presidency. However, the restoration of parliamentary democracy could not of itself create a democratic society. The government showed no inclination to reform powerful institutions which were suffused with undemocratic practices and a traditional bias towards the rich and powerful. Instead it followed the custom of filling many of the posts in public administration and the judiciary with its own political nominees. This practice sometimes rebounded against the government, as when AP vetoed the appointment of Javier Perez de Cuellar as ambassador to Brazil (because he had worked under Velasco) shortly before his election as Secretary General of the UN. Official currruption, which had flourished under the military regime, tended to increase, and Belaunde took no steps to purge the armed forces or punish individual officers for the excesses and abuses of the military regime.

Belaunde's first act of government was to restore press freedom, dismantling the military regime's censorship apparatus, and returning the expropriated newspapers and TV stations to their former owners. The proprietors showed their gratitude with a largely uncritical loyalty to the government, bordering on self-censorship. However, an unrestricted, and often sensationalist, opposition press emerged, including three dailies: *El Diario de Marka, El Observador* and *La Republica,* which became Peru's largest-selling daily. However, the coverage given by the left-wing *El Diario* to human rights abuses by the security forces in their repression of Sendero Luminoso meant that its Ayacucho correspondents were subjected to repeated arrest, death threats, and harassment, including the dynamiting of the home of reporter Luis Morales. Current affairs programmes on television that were critical of the government had a chequered career, several being removed from the screen by TV companies themselves.

Meanwhile, the government's economic policies undermined democracy's social base by accentuating the chasm between a small elite and an impoverished majority. The regime responded with increasing intolerance and authoritarianism to the social and political protest these policies generated. As Sendero Luminoso's guerrilla war developed, Belaunde and his ministers launched sporadic smear campaigns against the Church, foreign development agencies, and progressive intellectuals, casually accusing them of subversive activities. Left-wing activists with no proven connection with Sendero became targets of systematic repression in the central Andes.

The government's disregard for social justice was symbolised in Belaunde's presidential style. This was graphically summed up by cartoonist 'Alfredo', who in *La Republica* took to portraying Belaunde standing on a cloud, wagging an imperious finger at an emaciated Peruvian far beneath him. While of unquestioned personal honesty, Belaunde cut an increasingly incongruous figure. He combined the vocabulary and visions of a would-be nineteenth century statesman with an apparent incomprehension of the daily miseries of the mass of the population, to which his principal answer was the building of roads.

The government initially attempted to pacify the labour movement through dialogue rather than confrontation. Labour Minister Alfonso Grados called for a 'social contract' in which earnings would be linked to increased productivity in order to reduce inflation. He institutionalised this dialogue in a Tripartite Commission, which brought together ministers, leaders from the four national trade union confederations (but not from the militant independent unions) and from private business. Grados, an independent, blocked PPC demands for the scrapping of job security legislation. However, less than one worker in eight was covered by the law, and employers often evaded it by the use of contract and temporary labour. Neither was private business forced to take back workers sacked under the military government despite previous pledges by Belaunde, who had been photographed embracing sacked miners during the election campaign. Although the teachers were reinstated following a strike threat by SUTEP, others had to take their cases individually to the Tripartite Commission, which ordered the reinstatement of only 135. The government also attempted to phase out the industrial community by offering workers an individual profit-sharing scheme in place of collectively-held share capital. To the government's surprise, workers in most firms voted to retain the shareholding.

Grados increasingly found himself at odds with his government colleagues. Belaunde infuriated the unions by drafting a tough anti-strike bill, and although it was quietly shelved in congress, it gave the CGTP leadership a pretext for walking out of the Tripartite Commission in 1981. They were under rank and file pressure to withdraw because the Dynamo had patently disregarded its side of the social contract, appearing to view inflation as a relatively easy means of reducing real wages and increasing business profitability. Given the highly monopolised structure of the economy, businesses were able to pass on the bulk of inflation-derived cost increases in higher prices. As Rodriguez Pastor accelerated the phasing out of food subsidies, Grados's position became untenable. Resigning in June 1983, he said that 'an era of sacrifice will be more successful if the sacrifice is shared more equally'.

Wages made a modest recovery in the government's early years, but this was more than wiped out by a 20 per cent fall in real terms in 1983. By 1984 average wages for blue-collar workers in the formal sector of the economy had fallen to two-fifths of their 1973 peak. Salaries of white collar workers fell even more sharply to just a third of their 1973 value. Moreover, those workers who incomes were determined in the formal world of collective bargaining were relatively privileged compared with the mass of the under-employed or informally employed. By mid-1984, only one worker in three was formally and fully employed while 62 per cent of the workforce was underemployed. A fifth of Peru's 700,000 industrial workers had lost their jobs by 1984.

As the disaster in the formal economy became all too apparent, some officials and the pro-government press began to claim that the figures exaggerated the scale of the recession since, they said, the informal economy of back-street enterprise was booming. However, a study by academics and labour ministry officials in 1983 showed that output in the informal economy was declining at a similar rate to its formal counterpart. This underlined the umbilical link between the two sectors: corporate giants used backstreet workshops as suppliers and sold part of their output through street vendors. At the same time, increasing numbers of workers were fighting for a share of the informal economy's cake. The ranks of street vendors and taxi drivers, car and shoe polishers, prostitutes and beggars swelled. Many of them were children, as whole families worked long hours to scrape together a subsistence income.

From Dialogue to Repression

Wages and working conditions were not driven down without resistance and strikes were widespread. However, the three one-day general strikes called during the government's early years were relatively unsuccessful. The tactics used against the dictatorship did not bring automatic success under a newly-installed democratic government. Nevertheless, as the government's economic policy began to be popularly identified as a cause of declining living standards, the unions were able to move on to the offensive. A one-day general strike in March 1983 called by the CGTP and the independent unions was widely supported. The CTP and the right-wing fractions of the CNT and CTRP, grouped in the 'Democratic Trade Union Front', were pushed into breaking their pro-government stance and backed the strike at the last moment. Belaunde's preparations for the strike resembled those of the dictatorship: a state of emergency was declared, and the pro-government media implicitly linked the strike to Sendero. As barricades and mobilisations in Lima shanty towns stopped the buses, four people were shot dead by the police in the Comas district. A further six, including two policemen, were seriously injured while, according to union sources, more than 2,000 people were arrested.

As the recession sharpened and government policy hardened, the regime increasingly equated strikes with the subversion of democracy. The deployment of riot police equipped with tear gas and water cannon, violently dispersing marches by striking workers, became an almost weekly occurrence in central Lima. As low mineral prices forced owners to close small mines, groups of miners marched to Lima to demand government help. In several cases they were owed months of unpaid wages, only to be met with official indifference and police riot shields. A thousand miners and their families from the Cata Acari and Canarias mines camped out in squalid conditions in Lima for more than a year before the government intervened with loans to refloat their mines as prices temporarily recovered.

The CGTP attempted a 48-hour general strike in September 1983. But it was hurriedly organised, and did not receive the backing of the leadership of the Democratic Trade Union Front. Reduced to 24 hours, its impact was limited. Once again, there were violent clashes between the police and strikers in Lima, with the police shooting one student dead. However, in March 1984, following the opposition victory in the November 1983 municipal elections, the unions mounted the most successful general strike since the days of the dictatorship. This time the 24-hour protest was backed by all the union federations. The government declared a three-day state of emergency. A week before the strike Belaunde sacked Rodriguez Pastor, whose dismissal had been amongst the unions' demands. The strike was almost total throughout the country, and because the bus drivers joined there were fewer violent incidents. But in a clash with the police outside the CGTP headquarters, Jorge del Prado, the 73-year-old secretary-general of the PC-U, was wounded when police fired a teargas cannister at his chest at point blank range. Miraculously, he was not seriously injured.

During the Belaunde government the trade union movement made greater progress towards internal unity and a new relationship with the left parties. Under the dictatorship, this relationship had generally taken the form of a mechanical manipulation of unions for party ends. Individual parties often 'controlled' unions through a handful of top union leaders who were party members, rather than through political support among the rank and file, which tended to reinforce sectarianism in the movement. However, from 1980 onwards these trends were partially reversed because the unions were no longer operating in semi-clandestinity. This allowed a new generation of union leaders to survive without the backing of political parties, and because of increased cooperation between the left parties themselves following the formation of IU. Although the PC-U retained control of the CGTP leadership, its influence was diluted by the admission of SUTEP and the miners' federation. The party also lost control of one of its strongholds when the bankworkers' federation elected a non-party leftist leadership in 1983. On the other hand, the CTP did not escape the political turmoil into which APRA was thrown following its 1980 defeat. Veteran leader Julio Cruzado was close to the Townsend faction of APRA but maintained control over the bulk of the CTP, despite being suspended from the party and removed from the CTP's presidency. Cruzado's influence with the bus owners meant that he retained a powerful role in determining the impact of a general strike. However, APRA began to direct its trade union work away from exclusive emphasis on the CTP unions and towards working within their rivals in the CGTP and among the independent unions.

Although the general strikes demonstrated that the unions remained combative, their collective bargaining strength was undermined by rising unemployment, the growth of the informal economy, and the continuing downward trend of real wages. By 1984, strikes were less frequent, and in factory after factory the unions were powerless to fight redundancies and closures.

Impoverishment and Social Disintegration

The prolonged cycle of economic depression which Peru entered in the mid-1970s, and which intensified in 1982, had a dramatic effect on the living standards of the mass of Peruvians. By 1984 real income per head had fallen back to the level of twenty years before, but the aggregate figures concealed a widening inequality in the distribution of income. While all but the small elite became poorer, impoverishment was concentrated in the sierra and the coastal shanty towns. Behind the statistics of falling incomes lay a grim human drama of suffering and struggle (see box).

The decline in health standards was in part a result of the low priority given to health care by both the military regime and the

---

The Health of a Nation

Peru is one of the poorest countries in Latin America, not simply in the cold terms of its GDP but also with respect to everyday issues such as health, housing and access to drinkable water. This poverty has an effect on most Peruvians even before they are born. The care pregnant women receive is wholly insufficient: only 49 per cent receive any pre-natal attention and only 30 per cent post-natal care. State hospital services are very scarce, the fees of doctors in private practice far too high, and the cost of drugs prohibitive for hundreds of thousands of women. Average foetal and birth deaths are 40 times higher than in Sweden, the incidence in rural areas being much higher still. The official figure for infant mortality is 120 deaths per 1,000 live births, 40 per cent higher than in Argentina. Again, the level in the countryside is significantly higher; in some areas the figure reaches 230 per 1,000.

The effects of the lack of care and malnutrition on the development of the embryo continue after birth with the substitution of breast-feeding with powdered baby food. Intense advertising campaigns by transnational companies, misguided advice from hospital staff, and the inflexibility of working hours for women have caused a widespread and hazardous dependence on this 'food'. Not only is powdered milk insufficient in nutritional terms, it also becomes positively and directly dangerous if not administered under hygienic conditions and with clean water, frequently not available.

With urbanisation and the expansion of commercial farming, access to an essential variety of unprocessed vegetable and animal foodstuffs has become highly restricted. Commercial propaganda in favour of packeted and often imported foods of low nutritional value has harmed consumption habits. Fish is the cheapest and most ample source of protein for much of the population, but increasing quantities are being processed into fishmeal and exported to industrialised countries as animal fodder and fertilizer.

The fall of purchasing power by over 50 per cent over the last ten years underlies widespread malnutrition. In 1979 average consumption of milk was only ten per cent of the recommended

♦

amount. In 1983 the minimum wage only paid for less than a half of the family food basket. In order to assure a family with three children adequate nutrition a Peruvian needed to earn at least 330,535 soles per month; the average wage was 273,314 soles. Moreover, this average is calculated from the income of that one third of the economically active population engaged in the formal economy. Those forced to subsist on the 'minimum wage' of 135,000 soles could explain why it was that in 1979 Peru had a death rate of 11.1 people per 1,000 compared with six in Cuba and eight in Chile. At the same time, life expectancy was 58.0 years, compared with 64.4 in Chile and 70.1 in Cuba. The official figures for calorie and protein intake per person per day of 2166 and 56.3 grams do not convey the reality in many working class and rural communities, where the figures fall to 1560 and 26 (the World Health Organisation requirement being 2490 and 56). By 1983 between eight and nine of every ten children admitted to the Children's Hospital in the capital were malnourished; in 1971 the number had been five.

In 1976 only 9.8 per cent of the rural population and 72 per cent of the urban population had access to piped water. In Chimbote, an industrial town of 216,000, the water supply is less than half that required, with factories receiving most of the short supply. As in many Peruvian towns, the Chimbote water carts pass every two or three days, providing water that is costly and often impure. Such a situation, combined with lack of adequate drainage and underlit, over-humid shanty dwellings, encourages disease. The incidence of tuberculosis is the highest in Latin America, and respiratory diseases cause over a quarter of infant deaths. An almost equal number die from diarrhetic illnesses, which is easily understood when one bears in mind that 60 per cent of all Peruvian children under five are malnourished.

In order to confront this situation the state spends a meagre 4.1 per cent of its budget on health. Moreover, most of the services are highly centralised: Lima, with 29 per cent of the total population, has 52.3 per cent of hospital beds, 72 per cent of all doctors, and receives 49 per cent of the ministry of health's expenditure. Such concentration effectively excludes some 40 per cent of Peru from proper medical attention. The state social security system, IPSS, provides separate medical services for those in formal employment and receives 30 per cent of the health budget in order to attend to 10 per cent of the population. The armed forces receive 12 per cent of the budget to cover 6 per cent of the population and, as a consequence, enjoy the best doctor-patient ratio in the country. The people who suffer from the inadequacies and imbalances of this system do not, as a rule, suffer from 'tropical' illnesses, but rather those that abounded in the cities of nineteenth century Europe.

Belaunde government. Although investment in health provision increased under Belaunde, it still accounted for less than five per cent of total state investment. However, higher state spending would in itself have had a limited impact on the nation's health when the living and working conditions of the majority were deteriorating so rapidly. Belaunde preferred to devote the bulk of state social spending to housing. His government built and sold by lottery 30,000 houses in its first four years, but many of these homes could only be afforded by the middle class.

The impoverishment of the majority was accompanied by a process of social disintegration whose symptoms included a weakening of social institutions and sharply rising crime and violence. Low wages encouraged corruption, while the cocaine trade spread its destabilising trail across the police forces and the judiciary. The shift of economic activity to the informal sector weakened both state control and the organisation of labour and capital. Many of the victims of the economic depression turned to crime; by 1984 there were 28 armed assaults, four murders and two rapes every day in Lima. As bank robberies and kidnappings mounted, the minimum conditions of physical security required for capitalist activity began to be undermined.

This social crisis was dramatically highlighted in the breakdown of two institutions central to the functioning of the state — the police and the prison system. The three police forces were riven by rivalries and indiscipline. Armed clashes between them were not infrequent, while scarcely a week passed without press reports of policemen themselves committing crimes. The police faced the twin pressures of low wages and Sendero Luminoso's attacks. Their frustration resulted in a strike in 1983; this was followed by the dismissal of more than a thousand policemen, but not by comprehensive reform measures. Bribery and brutality were also commonplace in the prisons, along with acute overcrowding and appalling insanitary conditions. The crisis in the prisons exploded into violence. Outside Lurigancho prison an escape bid ended with the shooting of eight prisoners and their hostage, an Irish-American nun, by police disobeying orders. Months later, a cruel and violent mutiny by six prisoners in the El Sexto remand centre, in which a hostage was burnt to death by the mutineers, ended with the apparently indiscriminate shooting of 22 prisoners.

Neglecting the Sierra

In his first speech to congress in 1980, Manuel Ulloa announced that agricultural development was to be the new government's economic priority. After thirty years of stagnation in agricultural production, Peru had become increasingly dependent on imported food (food imports had risen to US$411 million by 1980). Two Peruvians in five worked in agriculture, but they contributed less than 15 per cent of national income. The rural population of the southern sierra comprised the most poverty-stricken social group in the country. The key to halting the migratory tide to Lima and the coast lay in raising production, productivity and incomes in the countryside, and particularly in the sierra. However, there were differing views within the government as to how to halt the country's agricultural decline. The PPC favoured reversing the agrarian reform while the Dynamo wanted to extend their free market drive to the countryside, abolishing state control of pricing and marketing. Belaunde, as in the 1960s, saw the solution as being to 'extend the agricultural frontier' through a widespread state colonisation programme in the jungle.

In practice, government policy did not always mix these approaches consistently. The state monopoly over the import and local marketing of agricultural products was scrapped, except in the case of rice. Food subsidies were phased out, and price controls abolished for most agricultural products. These moves were intended both to reward the 'efficient' commercial farmer and to reduce inflation by increasing competition. But while the military government's food subsidy system had favoured urban consumers at the expense of farmers, the move towards a free market also held disadvantages for the farmers. First, rather than raising farmers' incomes, free marketing tended to benefit middlemen who often held an effective local transport monopoly and could dictate prices. The margin between the prices farmers received for their products and the prices urban consumers paid widened. In a typical case, oranges and lemons from Piura were sold in Lima at up to 3,000 times the farm price. These trends also meant that farmers' incomes tended to rise more slowly than inflation and the cost of seeds, fertiliser and credit. Secondly, local farmers frequently faced uncontrolled competition from imports. Although the government stopped subsidising imported foods (with the exception of wheat and milk fats), these still tended to be cheaper than local produce. This was partly because Peruvian agriculture was relatively inefficient with much poor quality agricultural land and little capital with which to improve it, but it was also because northern hemisphere countries heavily subsidised their farmers through support price schemes and cheap credit. Thirdly, the government's failure to combine price liberalisation with a support scheme meant that Peruvian farmers were sometimes penalised when they did increase production. With a bumper potato crop in 1981, for example, the price received by potato growers fell below their average production costs.

While annual agricultural output fluctuated wildly according to weather conditions, officials could point to an underlying trend of modest growth. Yet, this growth was concentrated in a handful of products (rice, maize, soya and chickens), and concealed a continuing decline in sierra stock-raising, dramatically aggravated by the 1983 drought in the south. Despite this, almost all of state investment in agriculture was directed towards the coast and the jungle, not the sierra. The government inherited several unfinished giant coastal irrigation projects which involved diverting Atlantic-flowing rivers by tunnelling through the Andean watershed and were of doubtful economic efficiency. All the same, it committed itself to begin work on further projects of this type. Indeed, it was not until Sendero Luminoso had dramatically illustrated the dangers arising from the neglect of the sierra that the government hastily sketched an emergency agricultural development programme for the south-central Andean region. However, this appeared to be both too little and too late to have any political or social impact.

The government's laissez-faire approach to land tenure and the problems of the cooperative enterprises left pending the pressing issue of land distribution in the sierra, which the agrarian reform had not satisfactorily resolved. The 4,000 campesino communities continued to be deprived of land, water, credit and technical assistance. Yet, the government's major agricultural legislation — the Agricultural Promotion and Development Law, approved by executive decree in 1980 — did not even mention the campesino community. The law restored a free market in agricultural land, frozen by the agrarian reform. It also allowed cooperatives to 'parcelise' their land by dividing it up into individually-owned plots. The free market in land meant that banks could require their loans to be guaranteed by a mortgage on land, opening the way for the dispossession of cooperative members who 'parcelised'. The government apparently wanted only efficient cooperatives to survive while the remainder would quietly revert to private ownership, their land being gradually re-concentrated through the operation of market forces into privately-owned commercial farms. In this, the regime could rely on the co-op's own deficiencies, which government policy did little to check. By mid-1984, around 35 per cent of the co-ops had been divided up. In some cases, co-op members were disillusioned with corruption and bad management. Since the cooperatives had been imposed from above by the Velasco government, it was not surprising that developing a cooperativist consciousness often proved difficult. However, subdivision was normally a response to desperate financial straits, with many co-ops paying wages months in arrears. In addition

101

to the general problems of government pricing policies and climatic disturbances, the co-ops had their own financial headaches, stemming from their de-capitalisation before the agrarian reform, the added burden of providing social security and medical care, and being unable to lay off labour when weather conditions decimated production. The sierra SAISs faced similar problems, and many were reported to have effectively disintegrated through a combination of subdivision and invasion by surrounding campesino communities..

The Amazon Jungle

For Belaunde 'the future of Peru' lay in the jungle; infrastructure and colonisation projects in the sixty per cent of the country lying east of the Andes were the president's most important single concern. For him the development of the Amazon basin represented the tapping of an El Dorado of unexploited natural resources, a politically painless solution to the problem of land hunger in the sierra, a means of reversing migration to the coast, and a patriotic imperative to tame and populate remote frontier regions. However, the jungle development drive ignored reality: less than five per cent of the Peruvian Amazon basin was suitable for agricultural uses, the region's forestry resources required careful and scientifically-managed development if they were not to be squandered, and the region already supported a population, both indigenous and colonist, which was large in relation to its exploitable natural resources.

The Peruvian Amazon basin is composed of two ecologically distinct sub-regions: the high jungle (ceja de selva) formed by the broad valleys and hillsides of the eastern Andean fringe, and the dense flat rain forest further east. Most of the soils suitable for agricultural use are in the ceja de selva, which accounts for only some ten per cent of the region as a whole. The marginal highway, begun by Belaunde in the 1960s, opened up much of the northern half of the ceja de selva, with mixed agricultural results. Coffee, tea, cacao, oil palms, fruit and, above all, rice and coca were successfully cultivated in the area. The department of San Martin became the country's most important rice production centre. However, uncontrolled colonisation in the wake of road construction resulted in the desertification of some areas of the ceja de selva.

On returning to office, Belaunde concentrated on the extension of the marginal highway southwards and the building of penetration roads, although his enthusiasm for linking these with the Brazilian road network to form a 'Trans-Continental Highway' was not shared in Brasilia. At the same time, the president pressed ahead with the colonisation of further areas of the ceja de selva and adjoining tracts of the low jungle, as well as encouraging large-scale capitalist activity in lumber, cattle-raising and fruit-growing projects. The Agricultural Promotion and Development Law allowed rights over jungle land to be sold to private enterprises, including foreign companies. One of the first companies to take advantage of this legislation was Central American Services (CAS), which bought rights over 280 square miles for timber and ranching operations. Registered in the Bahamas and financed by a Cayman Islands bank, CAS was reported to be linked to the Somoza family. Nine special development projects formed the spearhead of Belaunde's colonisation drive. With a total investment of US$550 million, these projects envisaged settling 150,000 families in the region, some of them in the new city of Constitucion in the low jungle, inaugurated by Belaunde in 1984. The special development projects were largely financed by the World Bank, the Inter-American Development Bank and the US Agency for International Development.

However, Belaunde's jungle plans overlooked the existence and needs of the 220,000 indigenous Indians in the Peruvian Amazon basin. The majority of these 56 ethnic groups lived in some one thousand communities, of which 623 were officially recognised. Their numbers had stabilised and in some cases grown over the previous decade, following a steep decline earlier in the century as the rubber boom and earlier colonisation drives deprived them of land and exposed them to diseases, such as measles, against which they had no immunity. The indigenous population traditionally supported itself by hunting and fishing and the growing of cassava and bananas in small cleared plots. This subsistence lifestyle was suited to the jungle's delicate ecology but required large expanses of land since plots were left fallow for up to twenty years to recover after two or three years of cropping. The Velasco government's jungle legislation partially recognised the rights and needs of the Indians. It prohibited land grants to commercial enterprises, and land titles were awarded to 303 indigenous communities. Titled land was intended to be sufficient for houses, rotational agriculture, hunting and fishing. Under Morales Bermudez the titling process slowed down, and communities were no longer granted titles over hunting land, which had been the largest element in earlier grants.

Under the Belaunde government land titling of indigenous communities was almost completely halted. The lands of many jungle Indian communities, both titled and untitled, came under severe pressure from the colonisation projects. Less organised jungle Indian peoples in the areas of the central jungle were in danger of ethnic extinction as they were forced into a marginal urban existence in small-scale commerce in the colonist towns of the area. Stronger groups, such as the Aguarunas and Huambisas of the upper Maranon, managed to resist colonist encroachment on their land, and were trying to control their own development and increasing insertion into the market economy. Yet all the jungle Indians faced discriminatory government policies, which favoured the colonist. Unlike the indigenous inhabitants, colonists were encouraged with cheap credit, free travel on air force planes to and from Lima, and free air-freight for their agricultural products. But even with these incentives, few colonists remained in the difficult conditions of the low jungle for more than a year or two.

Coca and Corruption

For at least five thousand years the coca bush has been grown on the lower slopes of the eastern flanks of the Andes and its leaves chewed by the sierra Indians to help them work in extreme cold on an inadequate diet. However, since the 1960s when the opening up of the ceja de selva combined with a rapid growth in cocaine use in the US, coca has rapidly expanded to become one of Peru's most lucrative, though clandestine, exports. Peru is responsible for around half of world production of coca leaves, most of the rest coming from Bolivia. Its cultivation is centered on the Huallaga, Apurimac and Urubamba valleys, covering some 15 per cent of the jungle land in agricultural use.

A small proportion of production is legally cultivated for use in the pharmaceutical and soft drinks industries as well as traditional mastication. The rest is converted into coca paste, the bulk being illegally exported from clandestine airports to Colombia, where it is refined into powdered cocaine for export to the US. In the cocaine industry, as in many others, Peru produces the raw material while most of the lucrative final processing and marketing is controlled by foreign purchasers. At 1984 prices, the value of Peru's export of coca paste was estimated at between US$150 and US$450 million a year. Its US street value as refined cocaine was more than US$3 billion, or almost a quarter of Peru's total foreign debt.

The cocaine trade has spread a trail of corruption though the police forces, the prison service, the judiciary, and probably the armed forces. Coca dollars have also propped up Peru's international reserves, and provided some of the finance for urban property development. The official policy of the Belaunde government and its predecessors has been to crack down on drug trafficking and promote the substitution of other crops for coca. A small US-financed crop substitution project was established in the Huallaga valley and backed by a specially trained police unit. This unit (UMOPAR) raided villages in the Tingo Maria area, its efforts being directed against the campesino small producers. The mafia who run the export trade either bought police protection or operated from a distance through intermediaries. Crop substitution efforts were also of limited impact since the US did not provide the substantial financing needed to persuade large numbers of growers to switch to less lucrative crops. As Sendero Luminoso moved into the Huallaga valley in 1983, the government's anti-coca efforts ground to a halt. Crop substitution technicians stopped their work in the countryside while UMOPAR turned its attentions to combatting the guerrillas.

7 Sendero Luminoso

The social disintegration set in train by economic depression found its most dramatic expression in Sendero Luminoso's violent insurgency. Few Peruvians took Sendero seriously when it began its armed struggle in May 1980 while the rest of the Peruvian left was occupied with the elections. Dynamite attacks in the central sierra in the months following the assault on the Chuschi polling station were dismissed by the government as the work of common criminals and seen in left-wing circles as 'dirty tricks' by the military intelligence services. Yet, four years later Sendero's guerrilla campaign and the repression it provoked were plunging central Peru into a civil war. This sharply accelerated the political polarisation of the country and threatened the future viability of parliamentary democracy in Peru. Senderista violence drew a much greater counter-violence from the security forces. In the remote and rugged mountains of Ayacucho, massacres, 'disappearances' and torture became everyday realities for the Quechua-speaking campesino population, but these methods failed to break the guerrilla organisation. Although by mid-1984 Sendero was largely on the defensive in its Ayacucho birthplace, it had spread its operations across much of the rest of the country.

Sendero Luminoso's ideological roots lay in a fundamentalist version of maoism, but it evolved into a home-grown revolutionary movement of the Peruvian sierra, drawing on ancestral traditions of indigenous rebellion against the 'mistis', as the white outsiders, the local representatives of the centralised state and coastal capitalism, are known in Quechua. These traditions acquired a new relevance for a disaffected generation of Indian and mestizo youth, whose education made them increasingly impatient with the old problems of land hunger and unemployment that the Velasco reforms had done little to mitigate in the sierra. Many of Sendero's political leaders were older white or mestizo intellectuals, but these youths formed the rank and file. Sendero probably had no more than 3,000 full-time guerrillas by mid-1984 although the number was growing. In contrast to the 1965 guerrillas, who appeared as alien intruders in the ceja de selva of Junin, Sendero took deep root in some of the campesino communities of Ayacucho. The organisation could count upon an irregular and barely-armed militia of several thousand peasants, who, working their land by day, could be mobilised for night actions in the neighbourhood. However, in this most unconventional of 'irregular' wars, the guerrilla made no effort to defend territory or protect the communities that supported it. In Lima and other coastal cities Sendero formed cells of students and young people, often of school age, in the shanty towns. Sendero's membership differed from that of all other Peruvian political parties not only in its youth, but also in the prominent role played by women in the movement. Several of the leading guerrilla commanders were women. In both the town and the countryside the party's tightly-organised cell structure rendered it remarkably resistant to penetration by agents of the state but also reinforced Sendero's internal authoritarianism.

Belaunde repeatedly described Sendero as part of an exotic 'foreign conspiracy', whose plotters were deemed to include Amnesty International, the foreign press, and the drug mafia, corrupting the 'traditionally peaceable' Peruvian Indian. Ministers also hinted at links with Cuba, China and the Soviet Union, but were unable to substantiate their assertions. Several of those who were to become leaders of Sendero visited China during the Cultural Revolution, but the group was independent of and hostile to any of the world centres of international communism. However, it proclaimed its support for the 'Shanghai Gang of Four' in slogans painted on the adobe walls of remote campesino communities. The guerrillas lacked the sophisticated armaments that international links could have provided. They relied instead on an intimate knowledge of difficult terrain, enabling them to attack at night and with the advantage of surprise. The limited numbers of rifles and sub-machine guns they possessed were robbed or bought from police, soldiers, or sometimes from the drug traffickers of the jungle. These were supplemented by ancient hunting rifles and carbines hoarded by the campesinos since the War of the Pacific. But Sendero's main weapon was dynamite, stolen from the mines and highway depots that dot the sierra. Campesino guerrillas used their traditional leather slings (huaracas) to hurl dynamite-stuffed Coca Cola cans at police posts.

Sendero Luminoso emerged from the tangled web of Peruvian maoist politics in 1970 in the ancient colonial city of Ayacucho, with a population of 70,000 and strategically located between Lima and Cusco. The moving force in Sendero's creation was Abimael Guzman, then a 40-year-old philosophy professor and personnel director at Ayacucho's San Cristobal de Huamanga University. The group's nucleus was drawn from what was originally the Ayacucho regional committee of the Communist Party. Following the Sino-Soviet split in 1964, this committee had been amongst those to join Bandera Roja, Peru's first maoist party, but Guzman broke with Bandera Roja's leadership, which he accused of neglecting preparation for the armed struggle. His newly-formed group inherited Bandera Roja's considerable political influence in neighbourhood, trade union and student organisations in the Ayacucho area. Under Guzman's leadership, Sendero consolidated its political control over the university and particularly the teacher-training department, which gave the party an important link with the surrounding Indian communities. Many of the university's students were the Quechua-speaking sons and daughters of richer campesinos and small traders from these areas. Their studies completed, they returned to the countryside to work for the party. In 1977, Sendero declared that its 'reconstruction of the Peruvian Communist Party' was complete. Abandoning activity in political mass organisations — it had lost control of the university in 1974 — its cadres went underground.

Sendero's decision to begin armed action in 1980 in isolation from the rest of the left and the popular organisations on the coast corresponded to its belief that the conditions for revolution existed and that the road to communism in Peru lay through a 'prolonged popular war'. In its view, the Lima-based left-wing parties and the leadership of the unions and campesino federations were contaminated by 'parliamentary cretinism' and 'revisionism'. Sendero, by contrast, said that it was applying the 'guiding thought of Camarada Gonzalo' (Abimael Guzman's nom de guerre), whom they described as 'the Fourth Sword of World Revolution', his predecessors being Marx and Engels, Lenin and Mao. Guzman was known in his youth as a brilliant student at the University of Arequipa, where he gained degrees in philosophy and law with theses on 'The Kantian Theory of Space' and 'The Bourgeois Democratic State'. As a professor in Huamanga University he was discreet and respected. However, his politics developed into a dogmatic application of elements of Mariategui and Mao, leavened by a dose of inidigenismo. What the movement saw as its debt to Mariategui was embodied in its full name: 'Peruvian Communist Party — for the Shining Path of Jose Carlos Mariategui'. Guzman mechanically concluded from Mariategui's analysis of the 1920s that Peru remained in the 1980s a 'semi-feudal and semi-colonial' society. For Sendero, both the Velasco and Morales Bermudez governments were 'fascist', engaged in the construction of a corporate state and the development of 'bureaucratic capitalism'. The Belaunde government was seen as 'the continuation of fascism' behind a 'masquerade of apparent democracy'. In 'Desarrollemos la Guerra de Guerrillas', a 32-page pamphlet distributed in March 1982 and Sendero's only substantial public statement since it began armed struggle, the Belaunde government is defined as 'serving the deepening development of bureaucratic capitalism in the country; that is, of the capital of the great landlords, the great bankers and the magnates of the comprador bourgeoisie, who — under the command of imperialism, principally North American — are those who oppress and wound our people'. From its characterisation of Peru as a semi-feudal society Sendero drew the conclusion that the peasantry, and particularly its poorest layer, was 'the principal motive force' of revolutionary change within a worker-peasant alliance which would attract the petite bourgeoisie as a minor partner. From Mao and the Chinese Long March Sendero derived the strategy of a 'prolonged popular war to surround the cities from the countryside'. Its goal was to create the 'Republic of the New Democracy', a peasant-worker republic to be headed by 'President Gonzalo'. The limited experiments in rural areas temporarily controlled by Sendero suggested that the 'New Democracy' amounted to a kind of primitive communism or a back-to-the-Incas liquidation of half a millenium of misti domination. This involved the rejection of the capitalist money economy in favour of barter, which still co-existed on a limited scale with monetary trade in rural Ayacucho. It also entailed the rejection of modern technology, seen as a tool of imperialist penetration with few benefits for the poorest campesinos. Instead, Senderista agronomists like central committee member Antonio Diaz Martinez — who having been sacked as a director of the agrarian reform programme during Belaunde's first government for being too enthusiastic — turned to the study and improvement of pre-conquest agricultural techniques, still practised in much of the sierra.

However, it was hard to recognise Peru as a semi-feudal country, and still less as being controlled by 'the great landowners' following the Velasco reforms. Although some feudal cultural vestiges survived, even the most remote campesino communities were linked to the market economy, and their cultural isolation was attenuated by transistor radios and village schools. Nevertheless, in choosing Ayacucho and the central southern sierra as the site for his 'prolonged popular war' Guzman showed shrewd judgement. Ayacucho and the neighbouring departments of Huancavelica and Apurimac formed the poorest and most neglected region of Peru, the northern half of what the country's rulers traditionally called 'la mancha india', the Indian stain. Annual income per head in the region was little more than US$200, and the average Ayacuchano could expect to live for only 45 years. The area had been ignored by governments in Lima for centuries, and state investment per head in the region was the lowest in the country. Nine dwellings in every ten in Ayacucho were without water and electricity in 1972. Ten years later, the 1.3 million people living in the three departments shared just 1,750 telephones. The majority of Ayacucho's inhabitants were Indian campesinos, scratching out a living in some 500 communities scattered over the bleak Andean moorland and in remote valleys.

The poor quality of the largely unirrigated land meant that the haciendas in the area had never been rich or particularly large, and the agrarian reform arrived offering little or nothing to the majority of campesinos. However, the ending of the political domination of the gamonales created a power vacuum in rural Ayacucho. Aside from Sendero, political parties scarcely existed outside the city of Ayacucho other than at elections. The campesinos of Ayacucho took little part in the organised peasant movements that erupted in the 1950s, but the area possessed a long history of periodic insurrections of great violence. Drawing on this history, Sendero proceeded to fill the power vacuum.

The Corner of the Dead

Sendero's strategy of 'prolonged popular war' involved three main stages. The first comprised armed propaganda and sabotage operations, aimed at the consolidation of areas of influence in the countryside, the destabilisation and polarising of the political system, and the forging of an experienced guerrilla army. The second stage involved the establishment of liberated zones, followed in the final stage by total war and the surrounding and over-running of the cities from the countryside. Between 1980 and mid-1982 Sendero put into practice the first stage of this strategic plan, carrying out hundreds of dynamite attacks in the Ayacucho area, and to a lesser extent elsewhere in the sierra and in Lima. Their main target was the 'corporate state' and 'imperialist technology' in all their manifestations — public works projects, electricity pylons, agricultural research stations, and agricultural cooperatives. At the same time Sendero staged selective assassinations of village mayors and officials, aimed at decapitating the state in rural areas. Rural traders, larger landowners and rustlers were executed after 'popular trials', their goods and lands being divided up among the poorer campesinos in proportion to family size.

The government's initial response to Sendero was to minimise the guerrilla threat. However, counter-insurgency policy hardened after the first Senderista assault on a police post, at Tambo in October 1981. Retired General Cisneros, Morales Bermudez's hard-line interior minister, was recalled as minister of war, and a state of emergency was declared in five provinces. The island prison of El Fronton was reopened to hold Senderista suspects, and the government enacted by executive decree a tough anti-terorist law, creating the offence of membership of a group which uses terrorism to achieve its ends and that of making a public apology for acts of terrorism. At the same time, a detachment of the elite Sinchis ('those who can do anything' in Quechua) counter-insurgency battalion of the Civil Guard was sent to Ayacucho. However, the Sinchis proved to be effective recruiting sergeants for Sendero. The poorer sections of the peasantry were initially not greatly troubled by the guerrillas, who restricted their killings to the campesinos' traditional enemies. By contrast, the well-armed Sinchis stole, raped and killed indiscriminately, and failed to prevent further attacks on police posts. As the police withdrew to the towns, Sendero gained control over two extensive tracts of rural Ayacucho — the mountains between Huanta and Tambo in the north, and the area on either side of the Pampas river in the provinces of Cangallo and Victor Fajardo to the south.

Two events during 1982 underlined the power and public support that Sendero was rapidly acquiring in the Ayacucho area. The first was in March, when Sendero took over the city of Ayacucho for a night and attacked the prison, releasing some 300 prisoners, of whom around a third were detained Senderistas and the majority of the remainder suspected of drug-trafficking (see box). The second was in September, when a crowd estimated at 15,000 filled Ayacucho's streets for the funeral procession of Edith Lagos, a 19-year-old guerrilla commander detained and tortured to death in Andahuaylas.

In the last months of 1982 Sendero varied its strategy in an apparent bid to accelerate political polarisation. The guerrillas combined attacks on Lima's electricity system with an attempt to impose a war economy on the rural areas they controlled. They reportedly ordered campesinos to sow only enough crops for their own subsistence, and shut down country fairs by force. Their intention was to cut food supplies to Ayacucho, and to this end they blew up a bridge over the Pampas river, severing the important Ayacucho-Cusco road. Yet Sendero's perception of the rural economy as semi-feudal led it to misjudge the significance of trade for the campesino communities. Their crop surpluses were small, but still enabled the campesinos to acquire essentials like salt, sugar, candles and knives, while fairs also acted as important social meeting places. As a result, the self-subsistence policy provoked increasing hostility to the guerrillas, particularly in more prosperous communities amd was played down.

The Assault on Ayacucho Prison

'Sunday, 2 March, 1982. Time: 7.00pm. Three people wearing police uniforms arrived at the house of Melquiades Acosta and requested him to lend them his Dodge D300 truck to undertake an "important secret mission". After thinking about it, Acosta consented on condition that he accompanied them, and he left with the three unknown people. On the way he was easily made prisoner by his companions, who tied him up and left him on the road.

At 11.30pm, in a synchronised operation, four groups of armed men aboard two trucks, one of which was Acosta's Dodge, entered and occupied the city of Huamanga (Ayacucho). The first group surrounded the headquarters of the Civil Guard; the second did the same with the Departmental Headquarters of the Investigative Police; the third made for the Republican Guard headquarters, and the fourth and largest surrounded and attacked the prison.

When the penitentiary's main door blew up, a series of detonations were heard in the city; at the same time the electricity was cut. The alarm was given in the various police headquarters, policemen armed themselves and tried to go outside. However, wholesale explosions and shots from various directions warned them to stay where they were.

The prison door was blown up with several sticks of dynamite and inside an intense exchange of fire took place. Meanwhile, another group of attackers entered the prison from the rear, using ropes and ladders positioned from Acosta's truck. Half an hour later the Senderistas had resolved the situation in their favour.

Masters of the prison, they sung their anthems, raised their red flag and freed 297 male prisoners and seven women, among them the guerrilla leader Edith Lagos. Half an hour later, and after taking charge of the weapons they found in the prison, they vanished into the darkness of the night.

As a result of the attack, two Republican Guards lost their lives and eight policemen were wounded. On the Senderista side, between attackers and prisoners, ten men died. It was a commando action which required detailed planning and which mobilised, according to official information, around 150 Senderistas.

The assault on Ayacucho prison stirred Peruvian public opinion not only because "after this, anything is possible", as one paper said, but also because of what occurred half an hour later in Ayacucho hospital, when a group of uniformed Republican Guards dragged three seriously injured Senderistas from their beds and dealt them a cowardly death in the back.'

Raul Gonzalez, *Debate*, No.22.

Sendero followed this up with a spate of daylight shootings of top local officials in Ayacucho. These created panic in government circles, and underlined the demoralisation and ineffectiveness of the 2,500-strong police force in the area. Belaunde responded by placing seven provinces under armed forces control in December 1982, creating a Military Emergency Zone (MEZ) centred on Ayacucho. Over the course of the following 18 months, the MEZ was successively extended to include 13 provinces in Ayacucho, Huancavelica and Apurimac. An armed forces task force, estimated at 2,000 troops including paratroopers backed up by six helicopters, was dispatched to Ayacucho. The army initially acted with caution, giving logistical support to the police who were then able to move on to the offensive in the countryside. Military chiefs admitted that they were hampered by defective intelligence. As Cisneros stated, in an interview shortly before the army was sent in: 'One doesn't know who they are and where they are, since they all have the same characteristics as the people of the sierra. For the police to be successful, they would have to start killing Senderistas and non-Senderistas . . . They kill 60 people, and at best there are three Senderistas, and of course the police will say that the 60 were all Senderistas.'

Sendero opted for a tactical retreat in the presence of the military, some of its cadres slipping into neighbouring areas while others simply lay low. Since Sendero's operations involved a popular insurgency rather than a war of defined fronts, the security forces were faced with an enemy they could rarely confront openly. Instead, from April 1983, they proceeded to apply the strategy forecast by Cisneros, and Ayacucho began to live up to its Quechua name of Huamanga, 'the corner of the dead'. Hundreds of campesinos were killed in raids on the remote communities in the areas previously controlled by Sendero. The victims were described in terse military communiques as 'Senderistas killed in clashes' or as 'campesinos massacred by Sendero'. Few prisoners were taken in these 'clashes', the dead were normally not named, and neither were their bodies produced. Brigadier Clemente Noel, the MEZ commander during 1983, explained that, 'we don't have time to identify dead Senderistas'.

The military also tried to win support in some areas by donating food, alcohol and medicines, sometimes working through ex-army conscripts among the campesinos. Some communities, particularly in the mountains above Tambo and the cattle-raising valleys of Victor Fajardo, turned against Sendero. As neighbouring communities took different sides, traditional land disputes were re-kindled, adding a further element of confusion and violence to the situation. Sendero sought vengeance against some communities that had turned against it. The guerrillas began killing alleged 'grasses' in 1981. As the pressure increased following the entry of the armed forces, several massacres by Sendero, or communities which supported it, took place. In the most notorious, 67 people including children were killed in Lucanarmarca. In parts of Huancavelica where communities were strongly-organised and affiliated to the CCP, Sendero issued death threats against IU campesino leaders. However, these communities successfully resisted Senderista penetration, although this didn't save them from police repression.

The security forces were being advised in counter-insurgency techniques by US, Israeli and Argentine experts. An Israeli mission visited Peru during 1983 to advise on security measures in government installations, and Peruvian officers were regularly trained in 'non-conventional' warfare in the US. Until the election of civilian president Raul Alfonsin small groups of military and police intelligence officers were regularly sent to Buenos Aires for training courses, and Argentine police officers were reported to have visited Ayacucho. It was therefore perhaps not surprising that in Ayacucho and the surrounding countryside 'disappearances' became daily occurrences in 1983, as they had been in Argentina under the military junta. Many of those who 'disappeared' were taken from their homes in dawn patrols by the security forces. The majority were never seen alive again, although sometimes their decomposing corpses were discovered on roadsides or in ravines on the outskirts of Ayacucho. The minority who reappeared spoke of torture as routine in a dozen military detention centres established throughout the MEZ. District attorneys were illegally refused access to these centres, the existence of which was officially denied. By February 1984 the Ayacucho district attorney's office had received 1,500 signed statements by relatives denouncing cases of disappearances. In quick succession four district attorneys were transferred, or resigned following threats after they had publicised their difficulties.

Several alleged Senderista massacres appeared, upon investigation, to be the work of the security forces. In the community of Soccos, south of Ayacucho, 31 campesino men, women and children were rounded up by the police while celebrating an engagement party in the village. They were taken to a nearby river bed, shot and crudely buried. Although 26 policemen were provisionally charged with the murder, a year later they had yet to be brought to trial. In another incident in the same month of November 1983, 300 people from the community of Sivia, near the Apurimac river on Ayacucho's northern boundary, were marched to the army base at Pichari following the killing of an army officer. The 54 young men among those arrested were never seen again. Independent investigation of disappearances and massacres was hampered by the military authorities, who were

Uchuraccay — The Unsolved Murder of Eight Journalists

At 6.00am on Wednesday 26 January 1983 eight journalists left the city of Ayacucho in a hired car. They were headed for the campesino community of Huaychao, more than 12,000 feet up in the Andes above the town of Huanta.

Seven of the journalists worked for papers opposed to the government. Eduardo de la Piniella (aged 33) and photographer Pedro Sanchez worked for the left-wing daily *El Diario de Marka*, while Felix Gavilan (26) was one of its Ayacucho correspondents. Jorge-Luis Mendivil (22) and photographer Willy Retto (27) were on the staff of the Aprista-leaning *El Observador*; Jorge Sedano (52) was a photographer from the popular *La Republica*, while Octavio Infantes edited a local Ayacucho paper. The eighth, Amador Garcia (30), was a staff photographer for the right-wing weekly *Oiga*.

They were going to Huaychao because three days earlier Brigadier Clemente Noel (commander of the Military Emergency Zone) had announced that the community had killed seven members of Sendero Luminoso with what Noel called 'courage and virility'. Noel's sentiments were echoed by Belaunde, who praised the 'gallant' act of the community. It was the first time that campesinos had been reported to have turned against the guerrillas, and the journalists wanted to confirm that the killers had not in fact been members of the security forces and that the victims were Senderistas. Later investigations appeared to confirm the official version, and established that three of the dead guerrillas were truant school-children of 14 and 15 from Huanta.

After a two hour car journey and an eight hour walk along mountain trails, the reporters arrived at the community of Uchuraccay, five miles south of Huaychao. They had stopped en route at the house of Octavio Infantes' mother, where Infantes' half-brother Juan Argumedo agreed to guide them as far as Uchuraccay.

In Uchuraccay, near the community centre, the journalists were battered to death with great violence by stones and axes. Their mutilated bodies were buried in pairs, naked and face-down, in shallow graves outside the community boundary. The bodies were discovered by a mixed patrol of police and marines commanded by Lieutenant Ismael Bravo that arrived in Uchuraccay on the night of 28 January. The patrol had been dispatched by Noel after other journalists in Ayacucho had become alarmed at their colleagues' absence. The patrol recovered one telephoto lens, twelve rolls of unused film, and some of the dead reporters' identity cards, but not their cameras.

In the face of a national outcry, Belaunde established a special investigative commission into the killings, composed of novelist Mario Vargas Llosa; Abraham Guzman Figueroa, an 82 year-old criminal lawyer; and Mario Castro Arenas, president of the journalists' association. In its report, the commission arrived at the 'absolute conviction that (the killing) was the work of the villagers of Uchuraccay', possibly with the help of campesinos from nearby communities, but without the participation 'at the moment of the massacre' of the security forces.

The commission concluded that the journalists were killed because the campesinos 'confused the nine strangers who were approaching with a detachment of Senderistas'. This was because they were expecting a revenge attack by Sendero according to the commission — the Iquichano Indians who inhabit the poor mountain communities of Huanta had decided in an assembly earlier in January to 'confront Sendero', whom they saw as a threat to what Vargas Llosa has called their 'regional sovereignty'. The commission believed that, in all, the Iquichanos killed 25 suspected Senderistas during January 1983, five of them in Uchuraccay four days before the journalists' arrival. However, the commission also concluded that 'the villagers' certainty that they had authorisation (to kill Senderistas who entered their area) from the authorities, represented by the Sinchis . . . played an important and perhaps decisive role' in their decision to kill the journalists.

A year and a half after the event, nobody has been tried for the journalists' murder. The Huanta judicial authorities in charge of the case said that they had not received cooperation from the security forces in their investigations. The government refused to intervene or to transfer the case to the Lima courts, on the grounds that the judiciary was 'autonomous'. Charges were finally drawn up against seventeen villagers from Uchuraccay, headed by Fortunato Gavilan, the community's lieutenant governor (the senior village official who although a member of the community, was also formally the local representative of the ministry of the interior). Gavilan, who was reported to be a former army conscript, vanished after an unconfirmed press report stated that he was taken into custody in the marine base in Tambo by Lieutenant Bravo immediately after the killings. Only three of the villagers who were charged were in custody, and by mid-1984 their trial had not begun. Court documents stated that the case had been impeded because the police ignored the judge's request to detain the remaining suspects and bring 81 witnesses to court.

A roll of film from Willy Retto's camera discovered by the

♦

investigating judge on one of his two visits to Uchuraccay showed that, contrary to the commission's 'relative conviction', the journalists talked to the villagers before their death. The pictures showed a tense confrontation, and that the journalists were frightened. But three of them spoke Quechua fluently, and would have been able to explain that they were reporters and not Senderistas. If they did so, either they were not believed or their purpose was considered to be equally disruptive.

The investigating judge concluded that for the community to have acted 'in such a cruel and horrendous manner it must be thought that it was incited by the police'. The Vargas Llosa commission reported that a patrol of Sinchis passed through Uchuraccay some time between 18 December and 26 January but since the commission did not insist on the security forces turning over their patrolling records, it could not specify the date with precision. Neither did the commission investigate a report in the pro-government *El Comercio* that 'a security force patrol' had left Ayacucho on 24 January 'to go to Uchuraccay to guarantee the security of the community' following the villagers' killing of five suspected Senderistas.

In subsequent attacks on Uchuraccay upwards of fifty of its inhabitants were reported to have been killed. Noel attributed these attacks to Sendero. They have eliminated important witnesses to the journalists' murder. A belated attempt by the investigating judge to reconstruct the crime a year later was abandoned when he found only one person in Uchuraccay, the remainder of its inhabitants having permanently or temporarily fled.

The possibility that the security forces were present in Uchuraccay during or shortly before the massacre, and that they knew of the arrival of the journalists, cannot be proved unless further evidence comes to light. However, the fact that the murders took place helped the military authorities to control information emerging from the rural areas of Ayacucho, hindering independent scrutiny of the security forces' conduct.

assisted by the murder of eight journalists in Uchurracay in January 1983 (see box), which discouraged other journalists from venturing out of Ayacucho.

As pressure from the security forces increased in Ayacucho, Sendero stepped up action elsewhere. By destroying pylons, the guerrillas blacked out Lima for up to 24 hours eight times in 1983 and the first half of 1984. Under the cover of darkness, they set fire to a Bayer acrylic fibre plant in a Lima suburb, and attacked police stations and banks. They twice staged raids on the Lima headquarters of Accion Popular, killing three people and wounding forty. The Bayer attack was followed by a two-month national state of emergency in mid-1983.

However, their 'dirty war' yielded some successes for the security forces in Ayacucho in 1983. They re-established more than twenty rural police posts, and regained control over the area around the Pampas river. Municipal elections were held in all but three provinces of the MEZ, despite Sendero's efforts to disrupt them. In Ayacucho Leonor Zamora of the small centre party PADIN was elected mayoress. She had campaigned for the withdrawal of the security forces, an end to the emergency, and a dialogue with Sendero. But in a demonstration of Sendero's influence, more than half of the votes cast were spoilt or blank, while AP gained little more than ten per cent of the total vote. With a lull in Senderista activity, Brigadier Adrian Huaman, who replaced Noel as MEZ commander in January 1984, announced a new strategy combining repression with social and economic development. Huaman, an Apurimac-born Quechua-speaker, pushed for an emergency investment budget of US$15 million, and attempted to tighten up police discipline. But his efforts to sack Civil Guard Commander Colonel Armando Mellet, whom local people singled out as responsible for many of the worst massacres, were blocked by the ministry of the interior. Huaman himself halted efforts to revive non-Senderista political activity in the area; an attempt by mayoress Zamora to organise a town meeting to discuss the pacification of the area was prevented by hundreds of troops.

The Final Solution?

Although Sendero was thrown on to the defensive in Ayacucho, it was rapidly spreading its operations to other areas. The police had some success in breaking up Senderista cells, mainly in Lima, but in general Sendero's tight structure resisted penetration. Although police chiefs said they had broken up more than a hundred cells, they captured only a handful of regional and just two national leaders (Antonio Diaz Martinez and Victor Raul Zorrilla), both arrested in routine checks. Luis Kawata, who subsequently transpired to be a central committee member, was released in 1981 because of lack of evidence. Sendero also survived an internal conflict during 1983, according to documents captured by the police. These revealed a successful struggle by the political leadership to retain control over the 'Popular Guerrilla Army' and the supporting militia. The documents also indicated a diminishing of the personality cult around 'Camarada Gonzalo'.

Guzman, who has not been seen in public since the mid-1970s and is believed to be suffering from leukaemia.

Sendero's struggle was also being reinforced by small left-wing groups. A faction of the MIR ('Cuarta Etapa') left the UDP and began armed action in the northern sierra of Cajamarca and La Libertad. Puka Llacta ('Red Land' in Quechua), a Bandera Roja splinter group, was operating in Pasco. Vanguardia Revolucionaria — Proletaria, headed by Andahuaylas campesino leader Julio Cesar Mezzich, had merged with Sendero in 1980, and Mezzich was reported to be an important Senderista military commander. A faction of PSR-ML was also reported to have begun armed action.

In June 1984, after several months of relative inactivity, Sendero and its allies launched a new 'offensive' over a remarkably wide area. In one month, 28 policemen and five soldiers were reported to have been killed, and Senderista bomb attacks or assassinations were reported in ten departments. As attacks mounted in the coca-growing Tingo Maria area of Huanuco, it became clear that Sendero had established a strong presence in the ceja de selva in the upper Huallaga valley. The government repeatedly referred to Sendero as 'narco-terrorists', but reports from the area indicated that the guerrillas and the drug traffickers were operating separately.

Belaunde responded by declaring a 'holy war against terrorism'. The government had ignored Huaman's attempt to combine repression with development, and had not made available the funds that the brigadier was seeking. Belaunde fell back instead on what appeared to be the last card of a strategy which failed both to tackle the economic and social conditions that were sustaining Sendero's insurgency and to halt the guerrillas' activity. He announced the handover of overall responsibility for counter-insurgency operations throughout the country to the armed forces' chiefs of staff, a move which he had previously resisted, mindful of his ousting by the military in 1968. At the same time, he prolonged a further national state of emergency (originally directed against striking SUTEP teachers and CITE civil servants).

A second MEZ was created covering the provinces of Huanuco, Leoncio Prado (Tingo Maria) and Mariscal Caceres (San Martin), and in Ayacucho; marines and commandos were sent to relieve the local infantry batallion, whose officers were considered to be vulnerable to Senderista penetration. These rear units formed peasant militias in communities, imitating Sendero's own methods. The militias were normally armed only with home-made pikes, slings and mock wooden rifles, and were ordered to mount vigilante patrols during the hours of darkness, with orders to capture strangers, alive or dead. Larger groups of campesinos accompanied military patrols on search and destroy operations against communities alleged to have Senderista sympathies.

The naval marines in charge of the Huanta area forced peasants from the high puna to come down to live under armed guard in 'strategic villages' on the lower slopes, causing considerable agricultural disruption and hardship. The strategic village 'experiment', very similar to that conducted in Guatemala, was part of a military effort to gain control through physical concentration and terror of that section of the civilian population which, the officers believed, had followed Sendero through fear. In many cases, militias were only formed after killings and house-burnings by military patrols. The new strategy served to reduce military casualties, but it exposed the peasants to Senderista revenge attacks and deepened inter-community feuds.

Establishing responsibility for the killings in the countryside was also hindered by the attribution of all deaths to Senderista action by military commanders and the government's information service. Nevertheless, Belaunde resisted military pressure to restrain the opposition press, and reports of human rights violations mounted. These included the disappearance of Jaime Ayala, the *La Republica* correspondent in Huanta, last seen visiting the marine headquarters at the town's football stadium. In August 1984, during investigations into Ayala's disappearance, government lawyers uncovered three clandestine graves at Pucayacu, near Huanta, containing 49 badly mutilated bodies. The only identifiable corpse was that of a 75 year-old campesino who had disappeared following his arrest by marines. As unease at the political cost of the counter-insurgency drive spread to some of Belaunde's own supporters, Brigadier Huaman responded with a public attack on the government's failure to come up with the money he had sought in order to finance development programmes. This prompted Belaunde to order Huaman's sacking as MEZ commander; he was replaced by his second-in-command, Colonel Wilfredo Mori, a Sandhurst-trained commando officer. Huaman had stated that the solution to Sendero's rebellion was 'not military' and that Ayacucho had been complaining of neglect at the hands of centralised governments in Lima since independence but, 'no-one took any notice and we're harvesting the result'. This opinion was shared by an important segment of the military, adding a new element of uncertainty to its relationship with the government.

In all, more than 2,500 Senderista attacks were registered by the authorities in the twelve months to July 1984; according to official figures, more than 3,500 people were killed between May 1980 and mid-1984 in the conflict between the security forces and Sendero. Unofficial sources put the figure closer to 5,000, not including those who 'disappeared'. Approximately 800 people were detained on terrorism charges, around sixty of them being members of IU. Less than fifty people had been sentenced for terrorism offences, and many of the detainees had spent upwards of two years in prison without trial. Of those killed, around 150 were police and some 50 were mayors or public officials, mainly belonging to Accion Popular. However, according to the president of the Ayacucho lawyers' association, 'the vast majority of the killings are attributable to the security forces, with the vast majority of the victims innocent campesinos.'

The Left Reorganises

Their crushing defeat at Belaunde's hands in the 1980 elections forced both APRA and the parliamentary left to reconsider their position. The convoking of municipal elections for November 1980 provided an immediate stimulus for the parties of the divided left to pull themselves together. They responded by forming an electoral coalition known as Izquierda Unida (United Left), which grouped together all the major parties with the exception of the trotskyists. Barrantes, in hibernation since the rupture of ARI, was recalled to preside over the new front and run for the important post of mayor of Lima. As a non-party independent, his nomination avoided party squabbles. APRA's electoral defeat, on the other hand, exacerbated internal strife. At the party's post-election congress in Trujillo, Andres Townsend and Luis Alberto Sanchez, another veteran leader, staged a walk-out with 200 delegates after Villanueva's nominee was elected secretary-general. Though Sanchez soon returned to the fold, Townsend organised a rival 'Movement of the Aprista Bases' (later to become the 'Partido Hayista') and was expelled from APRA shortly after the municipal poll.

The November 1980 election results gave victory to Accion Popular, both in Lima and nationally, but the left made important gains in the poll as the government's economic policy began to erode its support (see Appendix for results). IU came second in Lima, and won Arequipa and five other departmental capitals, mainly in the south of the country. APRA's vote slumped to 23 per cent, this second defeat compounding the party's crisis. This was not resolved until September 1982 when Alan Garcia, a youthful deputy from Lima was elected secretary-general, leapfrogging over the party's divided senior leadership. Garcia had been picked out by Haya de la Torre as a future leader, and had been Villanueva's campaign manager in 1980. He owed his election to the support of the octagenarian conservative

Sanchez, and to APRA's need to present a fresher, cleaner image. Garcia, who both physically and politically resembled Spain's Felipe Gonzalez, steered APRA towards a moderate social democracy. Advised by the Socialist International, Garcia dropped the more aggressively sectarian symbols and discourse of APRA's past and the party attempted to present a more open, united and democratic image. His election also signified the abandoning of Villanueva's effort to seek an opening to the left for APRA. The ascendancy of the centre-right within the party was underlined when Garcia was selected as APRA's 1985 presidential candidate, with Sanchez as his first vice-presidential candidate.

The first opportunity for APRA to demonstrate its recovery came in the 1983 municipal elections. Both APRA and IU attempted to turn these into a plebiscite on the government's economic policy. The poll gave the opposition parties a clear victory and underlined the government's unpopularity. APRA gained the largest share of the vote (33 per cent), closely followed by IU (29 per cent). Accion Popular's vote sunk to 17 per cent while the PPC gained 14 per cent. APRA secured its traditional base in the north but also won in both Arequipa and Tacna for the first time, being helped by divisions within IU in those areas. However, IU achieved a political breakthrough with the election of Barrantes as mayor of Lima, winning 34 per cent of the vote. The front made a clean sweep of all the capital's shanty town districts as well as most of the inner-city working class and lower middle class areas. With the PPC winning all of the upper middle class districts, Lima's political map became sharply polarised. Elsewhere, IU won control of Cusco and Huancayo.

After a decade during which the left had engaged in the politics of protest, it now faced the new challenge of important administrative responsibilities. Its record during the first six months in office in the Lima municipality was mixed. The council successfully launched an emergency programme to distribute free milk to pre-school children and pregnant mothers, and undertook other preventive health measures. However, it proved less effective at administering other municipal services, and despite its electoral success IU faced unresolved internal problems. The effort to mould its component parties into a cohesive political force was largely unsuccessful. The front lacked both an independent secretariat and a unified organisation at both national and local level. It remained merely a coordination system for its member parties. While the parties associated with the UDP took an important step towards greater organisational unity on the left when they merged into the Partido Unificado Mariateguista (PUM) in 1984, IU remained divided between often warring blocks. It found itself under conflicting political pressures from Sendero and from the right to which it did not always respond with a united voice. Attempts by the government parties and their supporters in the press to link IU with 'terrorism' were met with ever stronger condemnations of Sendero by Barrantes in particular. While PUM deputy Javier Diez Canseco repeatedly denounced both the 'militarisation' of democracy and human rights violations by the security forces, taking cases of 'disappearances' to the United Nations, Barrantes gave his backing to Belaunde's order to the armed forces to take over counter-insurgency policies. Barrantes' efforts to appear as a responsible statesman within the limits of the parliamentary system gained him support among middle class voters, but also provided political capital for those, like Sendero, whose message to the disaffected poor centred on the failure of parliamentary democracy to provide material benefits.

In a wider sense, IU faced a double political dilemma which it showed few signs of being able to resolve. Its constituent parties' growth in the 1970s had been based on a parallel rise in popular organisation, particularly in the trade unions. However, as the unions and other interest groups themselves fell victim to the economic crisis, the left parties found contact with their social base increasingly difficult. The left retained a powerful voice in the regional defence fronts, whose local strikes continued to be a feature of Peruvian politics. Yet as the economic crisis intensified this kind of protest politics brought diminishing returns, and as the organisational map of Peruvian society itself fractured, the largely white, Limeno and male leaders of the left parties were not always well-equipped to respond.

The electoral emphasis which the formation of IU and its successes gave to the left was equally problematic since there were powerful reasons to suppose that neither the armed forces nor the US would permit the left-wing forces grouped in IU to win a poll and exercise national power through the electoral system. The fate of the Allende government in Chile and statements from Peruvian military officers, who made little distinction between IU and Sendero, tended to reinforce this supposition.

Paths to Poverty

In Peru, perhaps more than in any other South American country, the economic depression of the early 1980s and the associated debt crisis exposed fundamental internal weaknesses. The problems that Peru faced as Belaunde's presidency drew to a close were far from transitory. More than a decade after the ending of oligarchic domination, the new generation of entrepreneurs and the middle class had failed to find a viable strategy for integrated national development, a goal which remained as elusive as in Gonzalez Prado's time a century earlier.

It was doubtful whether Peru could simply wait for the next raw material boom to lift it out of its depression. Long-term forecasts for raw material prices were not encouraging, and Peru was reaching the limit of its exploitable natural resources. Moreover, even if a large jungle oil strike changed this picture, Peruvian history was littered with similar booms whose benefits had not been transformed into self-sustaining economic growth. Instead, such booms effectively blocked the growth of an industrialist class powerful enough to attempt the transformation of Peru into an integrated industrialised economy. When the state finally attempted to impose these policies under Velasco, it was in many way too late for Peru's fledgling and largely inefficient industrial structure to challenge the global might of the transnationals.

Despite their political differences, the Velasco, Morales Bermudez and Belaunde governments shared a common failure to generate internal sources of development finance (through higher taxation of the elite) which would have bought them a margin of economic autonomy. The resulting foreign debt and deficits in government finances deprived Peru of all room for manoeuvre when the world entered a profound economic depression, the Latin American credit squeeze broke, and the country became the prisoner of its international creditors.

The Belaunde government also shared with its military predecessors a failure to limit arms spending, which was responsible for more than a third of Peru's total external debt. This pointed to the continuing weakness of civilian institutions in Peru, a weakness that was accentuated by the failure of the Belaunde government to offer the majority of the population any tangible hope of material benefit, any stake in the system they had struggled to restore. Peru remained deeply divided between a small elite and an impoverished mass of workers, peasants, and the unemployed. Wedged between the two, the middle class was itself dividing under the impact of falling living standards.

Nevertheless, the most serious short-term threat to parliamentary democracy arose from the state's inability to tame Sendero Luminoso without declaring war on a large section of the rural population. As a result, Sendero's guerrilla war was fast becoming the largest rural insurgency in Peru since Tupac Armaru's rebellion two centuries ago. Yet, at least in its present form, it appeared to offer no more than a blind alley of violent protest to a frustrated and marginalised generation rather than an alternative path to national development.

Further Reading

Alan Angell, 'Peruvian Labour and the Military Government since 1968', University of London, Institute of Latin American Studies, Working Paper No.3, 1980.

Hugo Blanco, *Land or Death. The Peasant Struggle in Peru,* Pathfinder 1972.

D. Booth and B. Sorj (eds.) *Military Reformism and Social Classes: The Peruvian Experience,* Macmillan 1983.

Francois Bourricaud, *Power and Society in Contemporary Peru,* Praeger 1970.

E.V.K. Fitzgerald, *The State and Economic Development. Peru since 1968,* Cambridge University Press 1976.

Abraham Lowenthal (ed.), *The Peruvian Experiment. Continuity and Change under Military Rule,* Princeton University Press 1975.

Cynthia McClintock, *Peasant Cooperatives and Political Change in Peru,* Princeton University Press 1981.

George Philip, *The Rise and Fall of the Peruvian Military Radicals 1968-1976,* Athlone 1978.

Alfred Stepan, *The State and Society: Peru in Comparative Perspective,* Princeton University Press 1978.

Lewis Taylor, 'Maoism in the Andes: Sendero Luminoso and the contemporary guerrilla movement in Peru', University of Liverpool, Centre for Latin American Studies, Working Paper No.2, 1983.

Rosemary Thorp and Geoffrey Bertram, *Peru 1890-1977. Growth and Policy in an Open Economy,* Macmillan 1978.

Appendices

Appendix 1. Structure of Production 1978-1983

Sector	Percentage of GDP		Growth (per cent)				
	1983	1978	1979	1980	1981	1982	1983
Agriculture	13.5	− 3.0	3.1	− 5.4	12.7	3.2	− 8.5
Fishing	0.7	30.1	9.5	− 2.8	−12.3	2.0	−40.0
Mining	9.8	13.5	11.9	− 2.8	− 4.4	6.1	− 7.7
Manufacturing	21.7	− 3.6	3.9	6.0	0.0	2.7	−17.2
Construction	5.0	−16.1	3.7	18.1	11.0	2.3	−21.3
Government	8.8	− 0.5	− 0.5	1.5	2.3	2.0	2.0
Others (mainly services)	40.5	− 2.5	2.7	4.3	3.8	0.4	−11.6

Appendix 2. Index of Real Income 1978-1983 (1973 base)

	Wages	Salaries	Minimum Wage	Consumer Prices (annual % change)
1973	100	100	100	
1978	61	51	56	73.7
1979	64	51	73	66.7
1980	69	56	76	60.8
1981	66	57	65	72.7
1982	58	48	52	72.9
1983	43	36	52	125.1

Source: Actualidad Economica

Appendix 3

1980 Elections to Presidency, Senate and Congress
(percentage of valid votes)

Party	Presidency	Senate	Congress
AP	45.4	40.9	39.6
PPC	9.6	9.4	9.2
APRA	27.4	27.6	27.1
UI	2.8	3.5	3.7
UNIR	3.2	4.6	4.7
PRT	3.9	4.0	3.9
UDP	2.4	3.5	4.1
Independents & others	5.3	6.5	7.7
	100.0	100.0	100.0
Invalid votes & abstentions (% of electorate)	36.5	35.9	36.6

Source: JNE

Appendix 4

Municipal Elections — National Results
(percentage of valid votes)

Party	November 1980	November 1983
Accion Popular (AP)	35.7	17.4
Partido Popular Cristiano (PPC)	11.0	13.9
Partido Aprista Peruano (APRA)	22.7	33.2
Izquierda Unida (IU)	24.0	28.9
Independents & others	6.6	6.6
	100.0	100.0
Invalid votes & Abstentions (percentage of total electorate)	40.2	47.8

Source: JNE; Desco

GRENADA

WHOSE FREEDOM?

The US invasion of Grenada in October 1983 was a flagrant and direct violation of international law. The Reagan government's determination to suppress the Grenadian people's right to sovereignty and the shallowness of its justification for this position indicate a preparedness to escalate further the violence with which its mandate is imposed in the Caribbean and Central America. Grenada threatened the US because it remained stubbornly independent and sought to develop its tiny society on its own terms. The tragic collapse of the government of the New Jewel Movement simply provided the pretext for an invasion that had been prepared and rehearsed long before.

Grenada: Whose Freedom? gives the background to and outlines the substantial advances of the 1979 'Peaceful Revolution' and shows why it was repugnant to both Washington and the Thatcher government. It discusses the debate inside the New Jewel Movement, the fall of Maurice Bishop and the events surrounding the invasion itself.

Latin America Bureau

Available from **Latin America Bureau, 1 Amwell Street, London EC1R 1UL**

£2.95 plus £0.75 postage and packing
US$6.00 plus US$2.00 postage and packing
ISBN 0 906156 25 4   Publication April 1984